PAN AM STORIES

PAN AM

Acknowledgments

This collection of Pan Am memories would not have been possible without the generous contribution of ideas, stories, and editing support of the following individuals:

James Patrick Baldwin
Captain Dave Bridges
Jennifer Brock
Dan Colussy
Captain Don Cooper
Asa Cutchin
Joe David
Paul Dickinson
Pamela Feack
Linda Freire
Dona Fuller
Captain Robert Gandt
Tom Hood

Gillian (Jill Kellogg)
L'Eplattenier
Ray MacIntyre
Captain John Marshall
Gloria Milhoun
Captain Mark Pyle
RosieRosenstein
Al Topping
Edward Trippe
Jim Wilkerson
George Young
Carol Zoltowski

I also wish to thank the following organizations for their permission of the fair use of copyright materials for the express purpose of education and 501(c)(3) fundraising. All net sales proceeds will benefit the Pan Am Museum Foundation.

The Pan Am Museum Foundation
Charles Lindbergh Blvd
Garden City, NY 11530

The Pan Am Historical Foundation
PO Box 1065
Amherst, MA 01004

Duke University
John W. Hartman Center for Sales, Advertising & Marketing History,
Rubenstein Library
Box 90185
Durham, NC 27708

Dedication

To the family of employees of Pan American
World Airways and Pan Am
1927–1991

PANAM
Das größte
Luftverkehrsnetz
der Welt

FORWARD

Ijoined Pan Am at the beginning of 1970. My first position was Vice President Marketing Development when Najeeb Halaby was CEO and Juan Trippe was still Chairman of the Board. These were the exciting days when the 747 was first introduced to the world and I was honored by an occasional visit from Juan Trippe when he stopped by my office to discuss Pan Am marketing strategies.

Seven years later in 1977 the board of directors elected me President and Chief Operating Officer after I had served in several marketing positions up to Executive Vice President of Marketing and Services and as a member of the board of directors.

In the 1970's Pan Am flew to 120 cities in 83 countries with 41,000 employees scattered around the world. Additionally, the Pan Am Building was the hub of several of the non-airline subsidiaries that were owned and overseen by the officers and board of directors of Pan Am. These profitable subsidiaries included the Intercontinental Hotels, a chain of 82 upscale hotels located in many continents across the world founded by Juan Trippe in 1946 with the objective of being able to offer the best accommodations to our passengers. Pan Am Airways Guided Missile Range division, was the prime contractor to the US Air Force eastern test range operating out of Patrick Air Force base at Cape Canaveral, Florida for 30 years from 1950 to 1980. Pan Am provided maintenance and services for all of the rocket launches from the Cape. Falcon jets was another subsidiary which sold corporate jets. Its parent was a French company but 50% owned by Pan Am in the United States. Falcon jets was located at Teterboro airport in New Jersey and provided the first 14 Falcon 20's aircraft that actually started Federal Express (FedEx) in 1973. Pan Am was a pioneer in developing computerized airline reservation services. Our communications system connecting the 83 countries and 120 cities in those days was a unique technical achievement before satellites and other advanced systems were available.

But my distinct memory about Pan American was the high caliber and dedication of the Pan Am employees which really made Pan Am special . As marketing chief and then president I had the opportunity to speak to many Pan Am employee groups and I was always impressed with the questions and interest they had in the company.

As the Executive Vice President of Marketing & Services I was responsible for employees that presented the Pan Am image to the public and our customers including the advertising programs world wide, plus airport services personnel and the district sales offices in our various cities. This also included the food service department and the flight attendants who spent the most time in front of and servicing our passengers. We had the best in the industry by far. Our flight attendants were college educated, spoke at least one foreign language and had to meet rigorous physical requirements to ensure they could help passengers in an emergency situation and of course to look good as well. I realize today's environment would never permit those standards but it gave our flight attendants even back then a cache which made them stand out as being special. Their uniforms were always designed by top designers and always reflected a modern, upscale and sophisticated appearance. A courteous and professional image of Pan American World Airways was always the company's goal.

Our pilots were also the best in the industry. Our captains mostly averaged 10,000 to 20,000 flight hours of flying experience and had knowledge of airport conditions literally worldwide. We flew our modern and large aircraft into airports and cities many Americans had never heard of.

My years at Pan Am were very important to me and I still have strong positive feelings about my efforts spent working for its success. Its failure and liquidation in 1991, twelve years after I departed, was a major disappointment to me and I still wonder if it could have been avoided.

Without having any detailed information about the circumstances of its liquidation in 1991, it was somewhat surprising to me given that several US airlines including the majors like United, Delta, American and many others, all declared Chapter 11 bankruptcy in that general time frame; yet all reorganized and are now very successful airlines. The sale of the Pacific routes to United Airlines in 1986 well before the bankruptcy was a shock to me since I regarded the Pacific routes as Pan Am's family jewels: routes which Pan Am built from no air transportation across the Pacific beginning in 1934. Trying to compete with only Europe and Latin American routes had to be a real disadvantage. Finally, the Lockerbie terrorist act in 1988 was a sort of final nail in the coffin for Pan Am.

My comments only reflect my admiration and loyalty for the role that Pan Am played in the development of global airline transportation despite its eventual failure, which was due mostly to outside events beyond its control. Pan Am will be remembered as one of the world's most iconic and successful airlines in airline history. I am heartened that the Pan Am memory lives on in the publication of books like this one, and the continuous loyalty displayed by its hundreds of former employees that still support organizations like the Pan Am Museum Foundation, the Pan Am Historical Foundation, and other related organizations 33 years after the demise of this wonderful institution called Pan American World Airways.

Dan Colussy
Pan Am President & COO, 1977-1980

PAN AM

Contents

FLYING THE LINE

ANIMAL CRACKERS

END OF AN ERA

EPILOGUE

Preface

*P*an Am Stories: You Can't Make This Up—well, actually you can …
a little.

The vignettes you are about to read are all, as said in the movie business, "based on a true story." Some of the stories are 100 percent factual; others are accurate in the storyline and embellished for entertainment purposes—which is not to say the recollections could not have happened as described.

When people ask me, "What was Pan Am, and what made it unique?" I answer with the summary: "Pan Am was the first global international airline that spanned the world. Technically, Pan Am was to commercial aviation what NASA was to space. As an instrument of international commerce, it was often the first airline into a country and, in times of war and conflict, the last airline out. If you were overseas and the apocalypse was near, you'd call Pan Am to take you home."

This book is dedicated to the "family" of Pan Am employees, all of whom will tell you, anywhere in the world, that "Pan Am was family and the best job I ever had." These stories are meant to reflect the Pan Am sense of teamwork, camaraderie, compassion, commitment—and perpetual sense of humor that kept Pan Am in the air and in business despite the most challenging of economic, political, and violent circumstances.

Whether you are a former employee, customer, or simply an aviation fan of Pan Am, if this book brings a forgotten memory to mind, a smile to your face, or touches your heart, then it has served its purpose.

Ace Gilbert September 2024

PAN AM

AT YOUR SERVICE

Only God Knows

December tends to be the foggiest month in London and runs havoc on flight operations at Heathrow Airport. With only two runways for both takeoff and landings, prolonged fog will cause innumerable flight delays and cancellations among all airlines. Pan Am was no exception, and the passengers were bored and frustrated on this cold and foggy day.

Slamming a fist on the counter, the exasperated Pan Am passenger yelled to the passenger service agent, "When is this goddamn fog going to clear?"

Looking up from his Panamac console with the weary look of a parent whose child has now stepped on his last nerve, the agent replied, "Sir, if I knew the answer, I most certainly would not be working for an airline. I'd be the best paid meteorologist in the UK."

Shaking his head in disbelief, the passenger walked down the counter until he found a uniformed supervisor, who had a telephone to his ear but was not speaking. "Maybe you know what you're doing because no one else seems to," spat the passenger. "When is this damn fog going to lift so I can get home to New York?"

"Right, sir," replied the supervisor very politely as he placed his hand over the telephone mouthpiece. "I've presented that very question to God, but He has me on hold. Why don't you have a drink over there at the bar, and I will notify you as soon as I hear."

Mistaken Identity

Running down the very long concourse, the couple arrived at the San Francisco Pan Am departure gate out of breath, waving their boarding passes—only to see the white and blue "Clipper Liberty" 747 slowly pushing back from the gate.

"Stop that plane! Bring it back to the gate! We must be on that flight."

"I'm sorry, sir, we can't do that," explained the handsome and impeccably uniformed gate agent. "If we bring it back to the gate, the aircraft will miss the tightly scheduled takeoff slot, and all 250 passengers may be delayed for another hour or more."

"I don't care. Don't tell me that, you raging, arrogant, queen."

"I beg your pardon, sir," said the agent as he smoothed his lapel and adjusted his elegant Pan Am pocket square. "I may be a lot of things, but I am definitely not arrogant."

What's That You Say?

Ed and Dorothy arrived at Heathrow Terminal 3 to check in to their Pan Am 747 nonstop "Polar Flight" to San Francisco. They were giddy with excitement, and Ed did his best to keep a lid on Dorothy's enthusiasm.

It was a slow day for Pan Am; the summer rush was over, and passenger loads from Heathrow to the United States were low. With fewer passengers to check in, passenger service agents started to slip into boredom. Idle hands are the devil's workshop, and Ed and Dorothy were about to be the latest tools. The check in agent saw fresh meat with this retired couple and waved Dorothy over to his kiosk.

"Good morning, my lovely," cooed the agent. "And where are we going today?"

"San Francisco!" blurted out Dorothy. "It's our first time and we are so excited. Have you been there? What's a good restaurant? What sights should we see?"

"Come, come, Dorothy," soothed Ed. "Don't pepper the poor man with questions. Just let him do his job."

"No worry, sir. I am also very excited today because we are introducing a new technology that is voice activated. I will ask you a series of questions. You just speak into the speakers here facing you, and the computer will do the rest."

Speakers? Ed quietly questioned in his mind. *I've assembled stereo kits, and these are not speakers. They look like ventilation air fan grill slots to me.*

Dorothy was all in. "What would you like to know, young man?"

"Do you prefer the smoking or nonsmoking section?"

"Nonsmoking, please," replied Dorothy to the agent.

"Please speak directly into the speakers, madam."

"NONSMOKING, PLEASE."

"Aisle or window seats?"

"WINDOW, PLEASE."

"And you, sir, what seat would you like?"

"NEXT TO MY WIFE … is that too much information for the computer?"

"Not at all, sir," smiled the agent as he quietly keyed in the data on his keyboard, out of sight of the passengers.

And then, magically, the box behind the desk spat out two perfectly printed boarding passes.

"Here you go, sir and madam." The agent inserted the boarding passes into a crisp blue Pan Am ticket jacket, stapled the checked luggage receipts to the jacket, and directed them to the security gates.

"Isn't that marvelous, Ed? I can't wait to tell our friends about this new technology when we return."

"Best not, my love," smiled Ed. "They'd never believe us anyway."

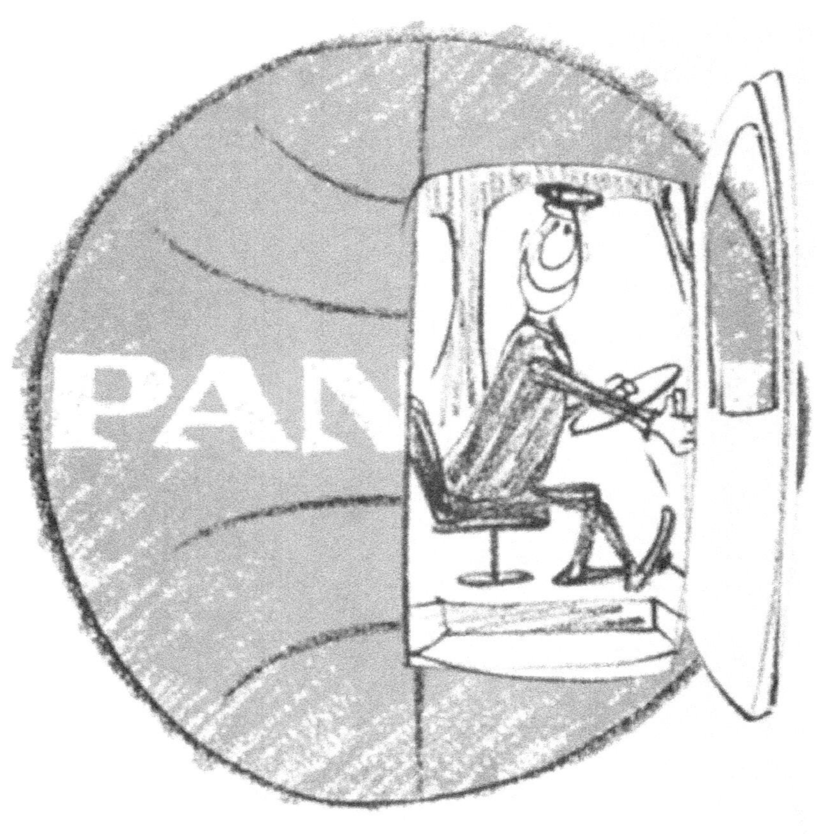
PAN

You Get What You Pay For

Washington Dulles Airport (IAD) opened in 1962 and was unlike any other airport both in its unique design and functionality. The main terminal was beautifully designed by Finnish architect Eero Saarinen in a similar wing-shape fashion to his design of the TWA Flight Center, which also opened in 1962 at what was then known as Idlewild Airport.

Unlike normal airline terminals of the day, where passengers boarded the aircraft from the terminal, aircraft were stationed at subterminals out on the expansive tarmac. To access those gates, passengers would board a motorized mobile lounge through a gate portal that looked very much like a boarding gate to an aircraft. Once aboard, the interior of the mobile lounge resembled a jet aircraft interior, complete with aircraft-size recessed windows. It accommodated 102 passengers but seated only 71, thereby leaving the remainder to stand and secure their place with a leather strap that hung from the ceiling railings.

The Pan Am passenger, returning to London and new to the Dulles mobile lounge experience, was having none of it. Having spent much of his waiting time in the terminal bar, he was well into his cups by the time he boarded what he thought was the Pan Am Clipper. Standing there, hanging onto a leather strap, he looked around and remarked to no one in particular, "This is ridiculous. I know I paid a cheap fare for this flight, but I'll be goddamned if I'm standing up all the way to London."

Bless Me, Father

In 1978, Congress passed the Airline Deregulation Act, which turned the US commercial airline industry upside down and inside out. Until then, the industry was regulated by the Civil Aeronautics Board (CAB), which determined which airline could fly where and how much to charge for fares. Air travel was treated like a public utility.

Now, any airline could enter or exit the marketplace, fly virtually anywhere in the United States they chose, and charge any fare they thought the market would bear. For Pan Am, deregulation was bad news and good news. The bad news: Pan Am's international routes were no longer protected from domestic airline competition (although such protection had been evaporating for years). The good news: Pan Am, previously denied the rights to fly domestically within the United States, now was free to fly wherever it liked to bring travelers to their international gateways such as New York, Miami, and San Francisco.

To compete with domestic rivals now flying overseas (Continental, Delta, American), Pan Am had to act quickly, and the chairman and CEO, William Sewell, a former US Air Force general, was accustomed to giving orders, not negotiating deals. Instead of expanding Pan Am with new aircraft and pilots, he wanted to acquire an existing airline in turnkey fashion. The Pan Am board of directors set their sights on Florida-based National Airlines to be acquired for cash that sat in treasury as a result of an exceptionally profitable year in 1978. The acquisition was like a shotgun wedding, and like most such unions, the marriage was hasty and poorly planned.

Training of the very different National and Pan Am reservation agents was done almost overnight in a slapdash fashion. National agents were expected to know global destinations seldom heard of, and Pan Am agents were expected to sell domestic cities they only traveled to for family weddings and warm-weather vacations. Legacy National patrons couldn't understand why they needed a valid passport and visa to fly to Melbourne, Florida, and Pan Am patrons were delighted to learn that the longest range Pan Am 747SP could now get them to Melbourne, Australia, in only three and a half hours without losing a day crossing the international dateline.

Charged with selling this new airline to the travel agency community that accounted for the majority of Pan Am sales, the marketing suits in New York came up with the theme: "a marriage of two great airlines." The San Francisco sales team rose to the challenge and invited local travel agents to attend a mock wedding reception to witness the marriage between two uniformed National and Pan Am flight attendants. Officiating the ceremony was San Francisco's sales lead prankster, Tom Hood, dressed in a clerical cassock complete with crucifix and swinging incense.

As he passed the hotel bar enroute to the event ballroom, a woman stepped out from the bar and asked, "Father, would you hear my confession, please? I am truly troubled."

"I'd love to my dear" replied the Pan Am priest, "but I am just on my way to officiate a wedding. Why don't you wait at the bar, and I'll come to you in about an hour."

True to his word, and plied with a few wedding toasts of his own, the Pan Am priest found the woman still at the bar, nursing a drink. "Now, my dear," slurred the pontiff," I can hear your confession."

"Oh, that's okay, Father. Half of my sins I confessed to the bartender, and the other half I can't remember. May I buy you a drink in absolution?"

Death in the Family

Long ago, in a distant land, before today's rule of instant ticketing, it was possible for people to book travel reservations and not pay for them until the last minute. Added to that, once paid, many tickets were refundable. Both business and leisure travelers would book multiple itineraries on multiple airlines, often not canceling the unused reservations. As a result, airline traffic managers had to overbook flights to accommodate the no-shows. In some markets, particularly the Caribbean, flights were overbooked by as much as 50 percent. Once closed, a flight could only be overbooked by a supervisor who would do so only for a preferred travel agent or a retail customer who could tell a convincing story. Today was such a call.

"Thank you for calling Pan Am Reservations. How may I help you?"

A man with a very heavy Caribbean accent replied, very excitedly, "Me granmudda ! Me granmudda is *die-ing*. I need to reach Pottaspain right away!"

"I'm sorry. You need to reach a part of Spain? Which part of Spain do you need to reach? Pan Am flies to Madrid and Barcelona."

"No, no, no, mon. I need to reach Pot-A-Spain, Trini*dad*."

"Oh, I understand. You want to fly to Port of Spain. I'm sorry to hear of your grandmother's demise. I can reserve a seat for you tonight at 8 p.m. or tomorrow at noon."

"Not tonight or tomorrow. I need to reach Potta Spain December 21."

"December 21? That's three months from now and the height of the Christmas season. Every Pan Am flight to almost every island in the

Caribbean has been sold out for months. I can place you on a priority waiting list."

"No waitlist, mon. I'm telling you for true that me granmudda is *die-ing*."

"Well, sir, I'm confused. If your grandmother is dying, how do you know she will be with us come Christmas?"

"Dat's what I'm trying to tell you, me son. Me granmudda is *die-ing*, but she die-ing *slooow*."

Panagram

In the early days of international commercial aviation in the late twenties and thirties, the experience was financially limited to the wealthy and governmental officials. Based on the cost and adventure, a flight on a Pan American Clipper flying boat was analogous to a luxurious version of a flight on an Elon Musk SpaceX or a Richard Branson Virgin Galactic. Additionally, federal government air mail contracts further subsidized the profitability of the Pan Am routes to South America, across the Pacific, and for a brief period prior to World War II, across the Atlantic.

Due to the limited capacity of the flying air boats and the small frequency of flights, keeping track of passenger reservations was no more complicated than managing hotel reservations. The Sikorsky S-40 to the Caribbean and South American carried 28 passengers; the Sikorsky S-42 to Bermuda and Brazil carried 37 passengers; the Martin 130 and Boeing 314 to Manila and the South Pacific carried 36 passengers.

Following World War II, aircraft size and capacity grew to 50 on the DC-4, 56 on the DC-6, and 105 on the DC-7. By the time Pan Am entered the jet age with a passenger load of 189 on the 707 and 220 on the DC-8, the reservation system known as Teleregister, consisting of wall reservation boards, typewritten manifests, and international telexes, was overloaded and required a modern upgrade.

In 1961, Pan Am announced a collaboration with IBM to develop a computerized reservation system based upon the IBM 7080 Data Processing System. Located on the fourth floor of the Pan Am building, it ran twenty-four hours a day. Developed at a cost of 25 million dollars ($260M today), the system to be known as PANAMAC opened in 1963 and remained in operation until the company closed in 1991.

Over the years, the system was continually upgraded and expanded to manage passenger reservations, hotel and car rental reservations, and cargo bookings and served as the global communication hub between headquarters and 350 Pan Am ticket offices in 200 cities around the world.

For many employees, PANAMAC was their first introduction to using a computer. New hire reservation agents were required to attend a two-week training class, plus pass a proficiency test as grounds for employment. A passenger reservation was known as a passenger name record (PNR) and required the use of a unique combination of alpha and numeric codes that somewhat resembled an English sentence of abbreviations, not unlike today's text acronyms.

Special passenger requests were noted as WCHR (for a wheelchair assist), SPML (Special Meal), and UMNR (Unaccompanied Minor). However, there existed one category known as RMKS (Remarks) within which one could type any free text they wished. It soon became clear to a pair of clever agents—a reservation agent in San Francisco and a passenger service agent at London Heathrow—that they could use the Remarks field to chat back and forth in real time. To create a live reservation PNR would be against company policy, so they created a "subload listing," which was a PNR used for airline standby travel and would not remove any revenue seats from inventory.

S/BOND/JAMES MR

5*RMKS - HOWS THE WEATHER IN LONDON?
5*RMKS - DREADFUL. HOWS SAN FRANCISCO?
5*RMKS- SUNNY AND BEAUTIFUL. I HOPE THE WEATHER IMPROVES FOR WIMBLEDON WITHOUT RAIN
5*RMKS- HOPEFULLY. ONE DAY THEY MAY BUILD A ROOF FOR THE STADIUM BUT PROBABLY NOT IN OUR LIFETIME

Unbeknownst in 1978, the two agents had invented the first version of the internet and texting. Today it is known as Instagram. Back then we would have called it Panagram.

Can You Hear Me?

John F Kennedy International Airport (JFK) has always been and continues to be the busiest international aviation gateway into North America. Today, four major runways accommodate all departures and arrivals, but there were as many as six active runways back in the early days of the jet age. JFK was formerly known as Idlewild Airport, which was named after the Idlewild Golf and Beach Club that was removed to build the airport, opening in 1948.

Renamed JFK in 1963 after the assassination of President John F Kennedy, the airport was home to most of the jet age departures to the Caribbean, South America, Europe, the Middle East, and Asia. Unlike later airports like Washington Dulles and Denver International built in rural, lightly populated areas, JFK was hemmed in by the densely populated middle-class neighborhoods like Howard Beach to the west, Brookville to the north, Woodmere to the east, and Rockaway to the south. Depending upon the time of year, weather-driven winds, and length of runway necessary for a fully loaded jet on an eight-hour journey across the Atlantic, one neighborhood or the other bore the brunt of the roaring cacophony of older 707s, DC8s, and enormous 747s screaming over their homes during takeoff, sounding something between a hurricane thunderstorm and the apocalypse.

On a given summer evening, a call came into the Pan Am reservation line.

"When are you guys (roaring jet) … going to stop flying (roaring jet) … over my house (roaring jet)?"

"Sir, I can hear the jets in the background, and I apologize and am sympathetic. I can report the noise to the airport noise abatement line. What is your address?"

"I live in Edgemere in Rockaway but forget the address. Tell your pilots to stop flying over my house. I can't hear myself think, or hear my wife talk, which by itself is okay, but this is nuts."

"I understand your frustration, sir, but I have to ask, why are you calling Pan Am? We are only one of many international airlines departing JFK, not to mention the domestic airlines like American, United, Eastern, National, to mention only a few."

"That may be true, young man, but let me ask you this: does Pan Am believe in truth in advertising?"

"Yes, sir, of course."

"Okay, as I read the newspaper ads, Pan Am is the most experienced airline?"

"Yes, sir."

"And Pan Am flies to eighty-six countries on six continents, right?"

"That's also true."

"And Pan Am flies the largest fleet of 747s internationally of any airline?"

"Yes, sir."

"Pan Am is the largest international airline in the world?"

"Yes."

"And JFK has the most international departures and arrivals of any airport in the United States?"

"Yes, I believe that's correct."

"Then who the hell else would I call?"

Bermuda Is Where?

Pan Am began joint service with Imperial Airways (Great Britain) to Bermuda from Port Washington, New York, in June 1937. The airline flew Sikorskys, while Imperial Airways flew the C class flying boat RMA Cavalier. In 1959, Pan Am introduced the first jet service to Bermuda with Boeing 707s. In 1970, they introduced Boeing 747 jumbo jets and ceased service in 1991 when it declared bankruptcy.

Only two hours by jet from New York, Bermuda was a perennial favorite for young honeymooners from New York and Boston. The pink sand beaches and genteel British hospitality were relaxing respites from the wedding frenzy from which couples escaped.

Because Bermuda was a tropical island, similar to Puerto Rico and the US Virgin Islands, it was easy to forget that Bermuda, as a protectorate territory of Great Britain, was a foreign destination for which a passport was required.

The young couple from Great Neck eagerly arrived at Idlewild airport, ready to check in on the early morning Pan Am Clipper to Bermuda International Airport. As a special surprise, friends had arranged for Pan Am to cater a small wedding cake to be part of the couple's first-class dining experience.

"Good morning," welcomed the Pan Am agent. "Tickets and passports, please."

The young man handed over two first-class tickets and his passport.

The young bride stood there, staring blankly and empty handed.

"Sweetheart, your passport. Where is it?"

"What passport? You never told me to bring a passport. I thought we were going to Bermuda."

"I did. You asked me where Bermuda is located."

"Yes. You said Bermuda was in the North Atlantic, located off the coast of North Carolina."

"That's exactly what I said. So?"

"So I thought Bermuda was part of North Carolina. You never said it was a foreign country. And it's a two-hour flight. Who gets to a foreign country in only two hours?"

Fortunately, the wedding cake did not go to waste. Bermuda being the destination, the cake was enjoyed by the other honeymoon couples on board.

PAN AM

CELEBRITY SIGHTINGS

PANAM

Missed Opportunity

During the eighties, Pan Am's key US city bases for flight crews were San Francisco, Los Angeles, Houston, Miami, and New York. New York was always the prime location sought by many flight attendants. After all, it's the Big Apple.

Housing, based on a flight attendant salary, was always expensive, and as a result, apartments were often home to multiple members who made it work primarily because everyone flew different schedules and were often away for days at a time. While apartments in Brooklyn, Queens, and Kew Gardens were cheaper and closer to JFK Airport, most Pan Am-ers preferred the convenience of Manhattan for the glamorous restaurants, hot clubs, and Broadway. Also, Brooklyn and Queens were the source of married men with children, while Manhattan was the purview of monied men who were single—or claimed to be.

Many preferred to live on the east side of Manhattan, which was a convenient city bus or taxi ride to the Carey airport express, then located at the entrance to the Queens-Midtown tunnel. If running late, experienced Pan Am-ers pressed a few dollars into the hand of the bus driver in exchange for stopping first at the Pan Am Worldport, instead of the usual counterclockwise route around the terminals.

Stepping from her apartment building on a sunny summer day, enroute to her assignment from JFK to London, the flight attendant noticed a stretch limo with a pair of sunglasses perched on the roof. She knew they were left there by accident, so she tapped on the dark passenger window with sunglasses in hand. The window slowly descended. "Yes?" asked rock star Rod Stewart.

"I think you left these on the roof of the limo."

"So I did. Thank you ever so much. These are my favorite shades. I would have missed them."

With a smile and a wave, he raised the window as the limo pulled away.

A couple of hours later, the flight attendant was welcoming passengers at the front door to the first-class cabin. Rod Stewart, accompanied by his wife, Alana Collins, approached on the jetway. Rod Stewart stopped at the door and looked curiously at the flight attendant as his wife blithely brushed by as if she were the celebrity.

"Ah," he recognized, "the girl who rescued my sunglasses."

"That's me. At least you could have offered me a ride to the airport."

Rod Stewart looked around carefully to make sure no one was listening, then continued. "You know, love, I recognized your Pan Am uniform and your travel kit, and I thought to offer you a lift. But, you see, my wife and I were in a middle of a bit of a tiff, and to offer a lovely lady like you to join us in the limo would have been polite—but suicidal."

Do You Know Who I Am?

There is almost no end to the number of entertainment celebrities who favored Pan Am internationally and later domestically. Publicists who managed these VIPs chose Pan Am not only for the quality of service but also for Pan Am's emphasis on the guest's personal privacy and Pan Am employees' discretion. Anyone who came in contact with VIPs, particularly flight attendants, was carefully trained not to fawn over a passenger and to take great efforts to shield their important guests from the prying eyes and minds of other passengers.

Nonetheless, such attention to discretionary detail did not prevent Pan Am staff from having a little fun from time to time. The first-class section of the Pan Am 747 overnight flight from New York to Frankfurt was completely full. Sitting quietly by himself in seat 1A was Al Jarreau, at the height of his fame in the early eighties, enroute to Frankfurt to kick off a concert tour of Europe. Late into the evening as passengers slept, the cabin crew retired to the galley area to catch up on their own meals, chat amongst themselves, and rest.

"May I get a glass of water?" quietly asked Al Jarreau, standing at the galley entrance.

"Of course," replied the flight attendant. "You could have rang the call button. I would have been glad to serve you."

"Oh, no, I knew you were all catching some rest back here. I didn't want to bother you."

The flight attendant smiled and then couldn't help but grin with a teasing thought.

"You know," she started, "you probably hear this all the time. You look a lot like Al Jarreau."

"Really, you think so?" Al Jarreau grinned back.

"Yes, very much so, just more handsome."

"Oh, well, now I know you're pulling my leg. I really am Al Jarreau."

"No, I'm not so sure," protested the flight attendant. "Prove it to me."

"Hmm, let see," thought Al Jarreau. "How about this?" He started to sing softly "Morning Mr. Radio, Morning little Cheerios, Morning sister Oriole …"

"Well, that's a good imitation. What else you got?" teased the flight attendant.

Now Al Jarreau was ready to rise to the occasion and launched into his well-known repertoire in an unofficial a capella concert. It wasn't long before the other first-class passengers woke to the music and took notice. The cabin lights came up, and Al Jarreau moved to the front of the first-class cabin and serenaded his travel companions with his hits: "After All," "We're in this Love Together," "Tell Me What I Gotta Do," and many more. Naturally, the captain and the flight deck crew had to come down from the cockpit to see and enjoy what all the fuss was about.

As the morning sun started to rise with the Pan Am Clipper approaching Frankfurt, the passengers sang along and applauded the generosity of the musical star. Breakfast and coffee were served, and the first-class cabin was prepared for landing. Al Jarreau did not get a lot of sleep before his first concert that evening, but he gave the Pan Am flight crew and first-class passengers a night to remember.

Some entertainers are celebrities. Others are just nice guys.

Pan Am Beatlemania

Ed Sullivan had never heard of The Beatles. By happenstance, in 1963, he was departing London Heathrow Airport at the same time that the Beatles were returning from a concert in Sweden and being welcomed by a screaming crowd of young fans. Observing the hysteria at the young musicians, he knew a hit when he saw one and secured a commitment for the group to perform on his *Ed Sullivan Show* in New York. Just another rock n' roll performance, he thought. In December 1963, the Beatles hit single "I Want to Hold Your Hand" was released in the United States and held the number one hit parade spot for five weeks. Their first album, *Meet the Beatles*, was released in January 1964 and climbed to number three. By the time the performance by the Beatles on the *Ed Sullivan Show* was announced for February 1964, the Beatlemania hysteria was on.

The international jet age was born on October 28, 1958, when Pan Am flew the inaugural Boeing 707 passenger jet from New York to Paris. Technically, the first commercial jets were inaugurated in 1952 by the British Overseas Aircraft Corporation (BOAC) between London and Johannesburg with the De Havilland Comet. However, numerous accidents forced BOAC to suspend jet travel by 1954, and jet travel did not fly internationally again until Pan Am in 1958.

The emergence of international jet travel in 1958 coincided with a post-war boom in cultural sophistication among the well-heeled. The Paris couture houses of Cristóbal Balenciaga, Christian Dior, and Coco Chanel created the "new look" in 1957 that would carry fashion forward into the sixties and beyond. Pan Am transitioned its luxury first-class Presidential Service from the well-appointed Stratocruiser to the new 707's with catering by Maxim's of Paris.

What marketers refer to today as "product placement" to enhance a brand within another medium was back in the late fifties and sixties a very human-based craft known as "promotion" or "public relations." In 1958, TWA, then owned by Hollywood mogul Howard Hughes, was the airline master of engaging celebrities into their promotional orbit. The album cover of Frank Sinatra's best-selling album, *Come Fly With Me*, featured a dapper meme of Frank Sinatra about to depart on a TWA Lockheed Constellation in the background. While that album was released in January 1958, nine months before Pan Am inaugurated jet travel to Paris, Pan Am had gotten the message. Pan Am had to be the hip and cool international airline of choice.

The choice of Pan Am over BOAC to transport the Beatles to New York in February 1964 was driven by Dick Barkle, Pan Am Director of Public Relations, and Brian Epstein, the English musical entrepreneur manager of the Beatles from 1961 until his death in 1967. Both men knew that the arrival of the Beatles in New York and their appearance on the *Ed Sullivan Show* would be the biggest publicity event since Elvis Presley. Brian Epstein, the ultimate promoter and showman, knew that the arrival of the Beatles on America's shore had to be a hip and glamorous All-American spectacle on an exciting American carrier, not a stodgy BOAC landing.

And Pan Am stepped up. The 707 first-class section, normally twelve to eighteen seats, had been reconfigured to thirty-six seats to accommodate the entourage of the Beatles and their girlfriends (John Lennon was married), plus news correspondents from the four major networks and numerous print newspapers. Extra stewardesses were added to service both first-class and economy cabins. The seven-hour London-to-New York flight was a delightful cacophony of twenty-two-year-young Beatles chatting up everyone else in first class, posing with the flight crew, and signing their autographs to a parade of Pan Am menus passed up the aisle from economy-class passengers.

When the Pan Am Clipper Defiance landed in New York and stopped on the tarmac outside the International Arrivals Building (IAB), the four Beatles posed at the top of the flight stairs, where they were greeted by over three thousand screaming fans (mostly girls) crowded four rows deep on the open observation platform of the IAB. This was the second coming of the rock n' roll gods, and they had arrived on Pan Am.

The publicity photography was carefully staged so that a Pan Am logo was consistently in the background. The Fab Four carried and flashed their Pan Am flight bags at all times. The chaotic and entertaining press conference of Paul, Ringo, John, and George was filmed before the backdrop of New York Port Authority and Pan Am logos. Frank Sinatra may have promoted TWA on the cover of an album cover limited to people who purchased it, but Pan Am was photo flashed, television and newsreel filmed, and print reported to millions of people around the United States and the world and would be a publicity icon for decades to come.

Your Table Is Ready

San Francisco has always been a restaurant town. The quantity and quality of restaurants is a key linchpin of the tourism industry. Historically, there have been more restaurants per capita in San Francisco than any other major city in the United States.

Cofounded by talented and temperamental chef Jeremiah Towers, Stars opened in 1984 as a continuation of his fame as chef at Chez Panisse. Stars was the favored restaurant of the moneyed San Francisco elite and virtually impossible to book a table at unless you were a member of the Nob Hill gang, a politician like Willy Brown, or famed San Francisco columnist Herb Caen.

Enter an intentional and persistent Pan Am flight attendant who honed her negotiating skills managing elite first-class passengers, self-important senior Pan Am pilots, and bazaar vendors from around the world. She developed her craft flying the global skies for Pan Am from 1949 to the final days in 1991. In tow was her younger brother, whom she intended to share the Stars experience with on her birthday.

"A table for two please," she announced to the maitre d'.

"Yes, madam, and the reservation would be under what name?"

"We don't have a reservation."

The maitre d' looked back incredulously as if the woman just asked for a job as a dishwasher. "I'm sorry, madam. Our tables have been sold out for months, and we don't take walk-ins. Thank you for stopping by."

"No, no, young lady, you don't understand," she instructed. "I work for Pan Am, and Mr. Towers was a guest of mine on a recent flight from San Francisco to London. He was so sweet and kind and told me that I should come to experience Stars when I was next in town—and today is my birthday"

Jeremiah Towers was not always on premises, but he was that evening. As he walked across the dining room behind the maitre d' station, the flight attendant called out, "Oh, Jeremiah, Jeremiah, may I have a word please?" The clarion call stopped Jeremiah Towers in his tracks and drew the attention of the nearby diners, so he thought it best to address the inquiry.

"Yes, may I help you?"

"Jeremiah, don't you remember me? When you last flew Pan Am to London, you were seated next to Herb Caen. You both were very complimentary of our service and particularly grateful for our generous bar service. You were so sweet and insisted that I experience Stars, and here I am."

"I don't know. I fly Pan Am almost exclusively, but I don't remember you. Sorry."

Having noted that Herb Caen was dining with a date at a table situated to see and be seen by the patrons, she said, "Come with me please, Jeremiah," and she walked briskly and confidently to Herb Caern's table.

"Mr. Caen," she inserted herself, "do you remember me? I was your first-class flight attendant not long ago when you and Mr. Towers, here, flew together to London. Remember when Mr. Towers invited me to dine here at Stars, and you said, 'That's a great idea, Jeremiah, but I don't think your martinis will be as good as the ones our hostess is serving'?"

"That sounds viable," pondered Herb Caen. "Jeremiah, do you recall?"

"No, Herb, I don't remember any such story—and we just don't have a table available for this young lady and her companion."

By now Herb Caen was beyond his two martinis and was making short work of a bottle of wine.

"Really, Jeremiah?" smiled Herb Caen. "You can't carve out a simple table for two given all the free upgrades Pan Am has endowed us both with? Come on," teased Herb Caen. "I don't have a column for tomorrow's paper, but this could be a good one."

"Madam, if you would give me a few minutes and have a glass of wine at the bar as our guest, we will find something for you," hissed a tight-lipped Jeremiah Towers. All to prove the Pan Am flight attendant motto works: "Where there's a will … there's a relative."

Who Is That?

He was a relatively shy, unassuming young man from Minnesota who loved to fly. Starting as a circus barnstormer and then US Postal Service pilot in the first half of the twenties, he convinced a group of St. Louis businessmen to sponsor his attempt to win the $25,000 prize to fly solo across the Atlantic. His success in that venture led to instant fame, which he carried reluctantly, and he later moved his family to Europe to preserve his sense of privacy until the advent of war in Europe forced his return to the US in 1939.

With Pan Am founder and chairman Juan Trippe, he shared a mutual love of aviation and a strong passion that commercial aviation could both shrink the world geographically and bring people closer together politically. He also shared a kindred spirit with Juan Trippe for privacy and quiet diplomacy.

Together they made a good pair. The aviator was nicknamed "the lone eagle," while his friend Juan Trippe was known as the master negotiator.

The aviator served as a technical advisor to Pan Am from the early expansion days in the thirties until his death in 1974, and he often shared leisurely weekends with Juan Trippe and his family at their East Hampton home.

Juan Trippe annually organized overseas trips for the board of directors to inspect and enjoy the destinations that Pan Am had built and profited from. On one such trip to Singapore, Juan Trippe organized a side trip to Saigon in the early days of US military support of the Vietnam conflict and before the war escalated with the Tet offensive. In Saigon they were hosted and briefed by General Willian

Westmoreland, Commander of US Forces, who appreciated the logistic and transportation support provided by Pan Am in a war zone

The Pan Am executives consisted of Chairman Juan Trippe, CEO Harold Gray, and the aviator, who sat quietly at the end of the table and said little. As the meeting concluded and people gathered their papers to leave, General Westmoreland pulled Juan Trippe aside and inquired, "Juan, I recognized Halaby and Seawell, but who was that tall guy at the end of the table?"

"Oh, him?" smiled Juan Trippe. "That's Charles Lindbergh."

Souvenir Caviar

With the passage of the Airline Deregulation Act in 1978, Pan Am finally received long awaited rights to carry passengers domestically within the United States. One of the most coveted routes was between New York and Los Angeles; a route frequented by the entertainment industry anchored in both cities.

Pan Am first class was popular among the actors and executives of Broadway and Hollywood. The polished Pan Am flight attendants who serviced first class came to know the celebrities well by name and their special needs and habits. A Pan Am smile and professional attention were welcomed by the rich and famous.

It's always the hope and perhaps unrealistic expectation that celebrities who display a public image of success and financial security will behave with good manners and grace. And while that is more often the case than not, there is always the exception. The accomplished actress and comedienne Bea Arthur was such an exception on this flight from New York to Los Angeles.

Originally a stage actress, Bea Arthur later earned her recognition and success as a television actress on shows *All in the Family*, *Maude*, and *Golden Girls* and could afford to fly first class.

She settled into her first-class seat, exchanged pleasantries with the flight attendants, and requested a cocktail. After takeoff, the first-class cabin crew prepared the hor d'oeuvre cart that preceded the main course. The highlight was a large silver cauldron of chilled ice, within which a silver bowl of beluga caviar was stationed. Positioned around the edge of the cauldron were five or six small jars of caviar as decorative supplements should replacements be necessary. The flight attendant would offer a porcelain plate of crostinis topped with a generous portion of caviar, chopped onions, egg, and capers. The dish was accompanied by a small glass of vodka upon request.

The flight attendant was about to place the plate upon her tray elegantly covered by a starched white tablecloth when Bea Arthur held up her hand and said, "More."

"More of what?" asked the flight attendant.

"More caviar on the toast. And a bigger glass of vodka."

"Certainly," said the flight attendant as she piled more caviar on the crostinis until they disappeared under the caviar's cover. She added another jigger of vodka to the tray.

As the flight attendant was about to wheel the cart to the next row of passengers, Bea Arthur placed her hand on the cart and instructed, "Hold on a minute." She reached over and picked up all the extra caviar jars and placed them in her large purse. "You may go now," she dismissed the flight attendant.

The flight attendant smiled and moved on. Bea Arthur's traveling companion looked out the window in embarrassment as the wealthy and entitled actress enjoyed her caviar without a thought in the world.

PAN AM AT WAR

PAN AM

La Pecera

Operation Pedro Pan was the name of the organized exodus of 14,048 Cuban children from Havana to Miami between 1960 and 1962. The name was coined by *Miami Herald* reporter Gene Miller and was the largest twentieth-century migration of unaccompanied minors since the exodus of 10,000 primarily Jewish children from Nazi Germany to Great Britain between 1938 and 1940 in an effort known as the Kindertransport.

Not unlike the situation in Germany, Cuban parents were desperate to get their children out of Cuba. Fidel Castro had come to power on January 1,1959, and on January 3, 1961, the United States severed diplomatic relations with Cuba, which had expropriated over a billion dollarsworth of US agricultural, industrial, and oil assets, as well as aligned itself with the Soviet Union—a clear and present danger ninety miles from American shores.

Though born a Catholic and educated by Jesuits, Fidel Castro was quickly at odds with the Catholic Church in Cuba in part over the church's denunciation of communism and Fidel Castro's determination of an atheist state. He nationalized Catholic schools, shut down Church publications, and expelled many priests, including 132 priests who were rounded up in just one night and bundled onto a freighter bound for Spain. Ultimately, all religions were severely repressed, and celebration of Christmas was banned.

By 1960, Fidel Castro declared that the future of the revolution depended upon the controlled education of the children. He closed both Catholic and private schools and instituted a strict curriculum of anti capitalist, pro-communist doctrines designed to promulgate the communism upon which he intended to build the new Cuba. Based on both personal observations and political doctrines espoused by the

Communist regime, middle- and upper-middle-class families feared that their children would be brainwashed by a totalitarian education and even taken from their homes and sent to indoctrination camps. The exodus of children ages roughly six to eighteen began modestly in 1960 but quickly ballooned into hundreds per month between the failed Bay of Pigs CIA invasion in April 1961 and the Cuban Missile Crisis in October 1962, after which all commercial flights between Cuba and the United States ceased.

The majority of children were from Catholic families, and their transportation and visa waivers were arranged by Father Bryan O. Walsh, the Director of Catholic Welfare Bureau in Miami and initially assisted by Mr. James Baker, the headmaster of Ruston Academy, an American school in Havana. Father Walsh also assisted Jewish and Protestant relief agencies to transport 396 Jewish and 1,000 Protestant children.

When the American Embassy closed in Havana, the British government issued visas for children to fly KLM (Royal Dutch Airlines) flights routed from Havana to Kingston, Jamaica, where an entry visa to the US could be obtained for the next-day KLM flight from Kingston to Miami. Alternatively, another KLM flight stopped in Miami enroute to Kingston. Supposedly in transit with a British visa, a child passenger disembarked in Miami and did not continue to Kingston. A US visa was issued in Miami with preapproval from the State Department.

As the surge of Pedro Pan children outnumbered KLM capacity, an underground network of parents and supporters issued copies of US visa waivers that replaced the British arrangement. Most children traveled on Pan Am, and for almost all the children, this was their first airplane flight. There were two scheduled flights a day from Havana to Miami, one in the morning and the second in late afternoon. Pan Am's support of the program included blocking out ten to twenty seats per day for the Pedro Pan program. The Cuban government required the Pedro Pan children to arrive eight hours prior to the departure of the afternoon flight. Only one parent was allowed to see the child off. Once checked in and processed by government officials, the children entered a waiting area divided by thick, soundproof glass. It was called La Pecera, the "fish bowl." Children would later recall how painful it was to watch their parents waving, pantomiming messages, and crying as the hours to departure ticked by. Children were allowed only a small suitcase with two changes of clothes, a small personal item like a toy, and one book. Religious articles were forbidden and, if found, confiscated. La Pecera would later become a euphemism for the separation of families divided by ninety miles of ocean and connected only by the visuals of family photos and occasional telephone calls.

Originally, the Pedro Pan children were told that the separation from their parents was temporary and that they would be reunited soon. However, Operation Pedro Pan abruptly ended with the Cuban missile crisis of October 1962 when all commercial flights between Cuba and the United States ceased. It would take three more years for most of the children and parents to be reunited, with the commencement of Pan Am charter Freedom Flights in 1965 from Verdado airport to Miami. Although 270,000 Cuban refugees exited Cuba for the United States on the Freedom Flights between December 1, 1965, and April 6, 1973, some Pedro Pan children were never reunited with their parents and grew up with US foster parents or other relatives.

Pan Am Flight 422 from Havana to Miami was less than an hour, not long enough to make much of an impression under ordinary circumstances. But it did leave a lasting memory for virtually every Pedro Pan child who flew Pan Am. Over sixty years later, many survivors still retain their boarding pass as a memento of that experience. Embarking upon the Pan American DC6 turboprop airplane was their first step toward the United States. The name Pan American, the American flag on the tail, and the warm welcome by American flight attendants who spoke English and Spanish no doubt provided a sense of comfort and confidence that made the departure from their homeland a little more bearable. Plus the Dixie cup of Coca Cola and a pack of Wrigley's Chiclets helped Americanize the adventure.

Pan Am was historically unique in that it was the first American carrier into an international country and, on humanitarian missions, the last flight out. One story that exemplifies what made Pan Am special is that of a young fifteen-year-old girl, ready to depart Havana in September 1961. As she was about to climb the steps up to the Pan Am aircraft, the military guard stopped her, inspected her papers, and told her to step aside. She bore the name of a wealthy family, and the guard had been told by his superiors back in the terminal to detain her while officials verified that the family had transferred to the government certain property in exchange for permission for her to leave . As the little girl cried, the Pan Am flight attendant came down the steps and assured her that "it will be okay." Time slipped by as the departure time had passed, and the airport control tower insisted that the Pan Am captain initiate departure. "Negative," replied the captain, "I am missing one passenger." The flight attendant continued to hold the girl's hand. "It will be okay," she repeated. Forty-five minutes later, the girl and flight attendant were waved aboard. As they entered the cabin, the captain met them at the door and said to the frightened girl, "I was not leaving without you."

Six years later, that young girl, then twenty-one, joined Pan Am as a flight attendant, where she dedicated herself to passenger comfort and safety until Pan Am ceased flying in December 1991. Over the years, she held the hands of hundreds of unaccompanied children with the same comforting words: "It will be okay. We're not leaving without you."

Love and War

He was always lucky—the right place at the right time. He didn't pay attention most of the time to that blessing as he grew up in the Depression of the 1930s in Alameda, California, across from San Francisco, but he would appreciate it later.

When Pan American Airlines launched its "moon shot" of crossing the Pacific from Alameda to Manila in 1935, the young man didn't pay a lot of attention outside of the newspaper coverage. Eleanor, a young woman in high school, two years his junior and future wife and mother, commanded more attention.

The other interest that attracted his attention was aviation. As a runup to the war with Japan, the US government was investing a lot of time and money into training pilots, navigators, and mechanics in the art of military aviation—free of charge. Many of the local colleges and junior colleges were well remunerated by the government to train young men in these skills. He applied and succeeded in his aviation training requirements between 1942 and 1944.

By 1944, the war in both Europe and the Pacific was winding down to victory. The young man realized that his future rested not with the military but with commercial aviation. Based on a tip that Pan American was hiring, he applied for a position with the airline.

"I'm sorry, kid," said the hiring manager. "We're looking for candidates with a four-year college education. You've only got one. There are two guys ahead of you with four and three years' college education"

He convinced the hiring manager to give him an application anyway.

Luck would be with him.

When they completed their physicals, the four-year college applicant couldn't see, and the three-year guy couldn't hear. The one-year wild card was in. He joined Pan Am as an engineer on the Pan Am B-314 airboat Clippers in 1944 and retired as a 747 Clipper captain in 1981 with thirty-seven years in service.

By the mid- to late sixties, he reached the rank of captain and often flew the Pacific routes, including San Francisco to Hawaii and Guam, with occasional extensions to South Vietnam. Up until the North Vietnamese surprise attacks of the Tet Offensive and subsequent Gulf of Tonkin resolution, authorizing President Johnson to dramatically increase US troop commitments to South Vietnam, the war did not impact a lot of people in the United States. Now everyone knew someone from their local high school who was drafted to serve in what was quickly becoming an unpopular war. Such was the case when a popular graduate of the local high school was the first to die in Vietnam. Much to the disappointment and discouragement of the captain and his wife, their elder son decided to enlist as an infantryman, knowing fully well of his probable destination, and he was shortly shipped out to South Vietnam. Unfortunately for his parents, he wasn't much of a letter writer or communicator, so the best they could hope for was "no news is good news."

In June 1969, as he completed his assigned route from Honolulu to Guam, the captain was prepared to layover for twenty-four hours and fly back east. However, he was asked to extend his commitment by flying a Pan Am 707 cargo freighter from Guam to Cam Ranh Bay, a logistical distribution center south of Da Nang. He was personally opposed to the war, but he was a Pan Am professional: when you wear the uniform, you check your opinion at the door and do your job.

Saigon and all military bases were considered war zone airports. Pilots descended and took off at very steep angles to minimize their exposure as targets to Viet Cong rockets and light armaments.

After landing at Cam Ranh Bay, the captain taxied to the secure area where cargo handlers worked as quickly as possible to unload the stores and prepare the aircraft for a timely departure back to Guam.

As the captain met with the Pan Am dispatcher in the main office to prepare his flight plan, weather checks, and weight and balances order, a uniformed army sergeant approached and asked, "Excuse me, sir. Do you have a son, first name is Ross?"

"Yes, I do," replied the captain, uncertain if he wanted to hear any more. "Well, sir, your son just came in from the front with a POW for interrogation and thought, maybe by divine coincidence, you were the Pan Am pilot for the freighter. He's in the lounge. Would you like to see him?"

Another lucky day. The captain looked blankly at what he thought was the dumbest question he had ever heard and responded, "Of course, I would. How much time do we have?"

For the next hour, the captain and his infantryman son spoke privately and emotionally. There was no talk about politics and war—just family, friends, football, and gossip. Flight operations allowed the departure to be delayed another twenty minutes, but then the captain's first officer had to interrupt. "Captain, we have to go. The security window for departures is closing."

Back in the cockpit, the captain and first officer completed their checklists and prepared to taxi out to the runway. As he looked out his window, he could see his son on the tarmac—with a salute and then a long wave as he smiled goodbye. Neither father nor son could see the moisture in each other's eyes. As the Pan Am 707 lifted off the runway and banked steeply off to the southeast, the young infantryman climbed back into his jeep—and back to the battlefront.

Neither the captain nor his son knew if this was the last time they would see each other. What they did know was that they both were professionals; they wore their uniforms and did their jobs.

Shell Shock

The Vietnam war was an important part of Pan Am history, both for financial and humanitarian reasons. From the gradual buildup of troops during the late sixties and up to the final evacuation of Pan Am employees and families in 1975, Pan Am served the government in transporting troops and war materials and supported the soldiers in providing weekly R&R flights as a respite from the endless days of combat. Pan Am offered these flights at a token cost of $1 per month and at great corporate expense. For many battle-worn young men, the sign of the American flag on the Pan Am tail and the smiling hospitality of the Pan Am female flight attendants were as close to home as they were going to get until their tour of duty was up.

Pan Am also supported the troops when they got home by offering jobs to qualified pilots, machinists, and mechanics. However, it wasn't always easy to leave their past on the battlefield.

One such veteran worked in the auto shop, which was responsible for the maintenance and repair of all Pan Am motor vehicles utilized by the ground personnel: jeeps, tractors that pulled the baggage carts, and up to the massive pushback trailers and tugs. He preferred to work the early morning shift, as did his supervisor. When both were alone in the auto shop office in the predawn hour, the young veteran would often announce, "Incoming mortar fire," and calmly take shelter under the desk.

His supervisor, understanding the situation, made nothing of it and continued talking to the young man by reading the "discrepancy cards"— repair or maintenance orders for vehicles from the night before.

As the supervisor spoke to what was visually an empty room, the remaining crew would wander in, take stock of the supervisor talking to no one, and shake their heads. As those men took their stations, the young veteran would quietly emerge from his nest, take the discrepancy cards, and go about his work.

The rest of the crew thought the supervisor might be displaying an act of lunacy. Little did they know that he was displaying an act of kindness.

Behind the Scenes

Pan Am inaugurated round-the-world flights in 1947. Pan Am flight 1 departed San Francisco or Los Angeles and traveled west to Honolulu, Tokyo, Hong Kong, Bangkok, Delh or Karachi, Beirut or Tehran, Frankfurt, and London, terminating in New York. Pan Am flight 2 departed New York and traveled east with similar stopovers, ending on the west coast.

With that distance to travel and numerous stopovers, being able to fly the shortest distance between stops was critical to a profitable route. Between Hong Kong and Bangkok, Pan Am overflew parts of North Vietnam. In the early seventies, at the height of the US military presence in the Vietnam conflict, the North Vietnamese announced that their airspace was closed to Pan Am and that Pan Am risked being shot down if they continued the practice. Although Pan Am's 747s could fly as high as 40,000 feet, they couldn't guarantee that it was high enough to avoid an anti-aircraft missile. The United States government didn't know, and the North Vietnamese weren't telling.

Pan Am CEO William Sewell asked via mediary channels for the opportunity to negotiate an agreement. The Vietnamese government agreed, and the Pan Am Senior Vice President for Public Affairs was dispatched to Hanoi to resolve the problem. After cooling his heels for a few days in the Metropole Hanoi, as was the customary negotiating tactic of the day, he met with the Minister of Defense and the Minister of Civil Aviation. Meeting with the Minister of Defense was expected, but he couldn't quite understand why the Minister of Civilian Aviation was included. Perhaps it was because he was the one representative who spoke English—quite well, in fact, due to his studies at Stanford in the late fifties.

Discussions with the Minister of Defense around why Pan Am was not an extension of the "imperial US empire" and why Pan Am should be granted air traffic privileges over Vietnam went nowhere for a couple of days. The Minister of Civil Aviation said nothing other than translating the conversation. On the last scheduled day of meetings, the Pan Am VP had an idea and asked the Minister of Civil Aviation, "Tell me about Vietnam Airlines."

"Vietnam Airlines, founded in 1956, is our national airline for North Vietnam and is quite good. We provide service from Hanoi to Dien Bien Phu, Haiphong, Vinh Vien, and Dong Hoi. There is only one problem."

"What is that?" inquired the Pan Am VP.

"We have no commercial jet airplanes to service our growing civilian demand. We have only a handful of ancient propeller aircraft—Lisunov Li-2s and the Ilyushin Il-14 from the Soviet Union and Aero Ae-45s from Czechoslovakia. All are undersized and often inoperable."

As Pan Am was bringing online the new 747s at that time, the 707s were relegated to charter assignments, freight operations, and eventually retired. Pan Am had a surplus of underutilized 707s that were expensive to operate.

"What if Pan Am were to give you a 707? We would include training and spare parts. Would that be of interest?" After a few more rounds of horse trading, an agreement was reached: a Pan Am 707 in exchange for flyover rights over North Vietnam.

The deal almost crashed and burned. A few months later, as the Vietnam Airline 707 initiated its first trip with a full load of passengers, one of the four engines failed on takeoff. There was no damage or injury, but the Vietnamese government was furious. Pan Am quickly sent a replacement engine and a repair crew and, to fully make amends, donated a second 707.

For political and public relations reasons, the deal was never made public, and Pan Am 747s quietly continued their round-the-world itineraries safely over North Vietnam airspace.

A Flag of Convenience

Pan Am was a unique international airline in that Pan Am was often the first United States airline into a foreign country and, in many heroic cases, the last airline out. Pan Am started serving Iran in 1949 as it initiated the first round-the-world commercial passenger and freight service. Fifty years later, in 1979, Pan Am evacuated the last remaining American nondiplomatic citizens from Tehran to the United States following the abdication of Mohammad Reza Pahlavi, Shah of Iran.

The Shah departed Iran in January 1979, ostensibly "on vacation," but his need for cancer medical treatment was a well-known secret. Waiting in the wings of his exile in Paris, the Ayatollah Ruhollah Khomeini planned his triumphant political return to Iran and needed to charter a commercial aircraft large enough to accommodate his large political entourage and journalists and prestigious enough to command world attention. A 747 would do nicely, and the best in the business was a Pan Am 747. Ebrahim Yazdi, an Iranian-American physician living in Houston, Texas, who became a spokesman and advisor to Khomeini, reached out to Pan Am regional headquarters in Frankfurt with a generous and profitable proposal to charter a 747 with a full Pan Am crew. At the time, the Ayatollah Khomeini harbored no ill will toward the United States, and his party was negotiating very earnestly with the United States government to support the Ayatollah's return. If President Jimmy Carter could use his influence on the military to clear the way for his takeover, Khomeini suggested, he would calm the nation. Stability could be restored, and America's interests and citizens in Iran would be protected.

As charter negotiations and paperwork moved forward, Pan Am Chairman William Sewell was visiting the White House in an advisory role. Zbigniew Brzezinski, the national security advisor to

President Carter, learned of the pending agreement and lost his mind. He demanded that Pan Am cancel the contract immediately, citing only "the security of the United States" as the legitimate reason. When William Sewell forwarded his instructions to the executive office in New York, the president of Pan Am responded incredulously, "This is a strictly commercial agreement. What does it have to do with the security of the United States?" Chairman Sewell could not answer, and national security advisor Brzezinski had no interest in further explanation.

The deal was off. Ultimately, the contract and bright payoff publicity went to Air France. On February 1, 1979, the Ayatollah Khomeini returned to Tehran accompanied by 120 international journalists, including future ABC news anchor Peter Jennings.

Who knows what if any difference would have been made had the Ayatollah been pictured deplaning from an American flagged Pan Am 747? Would the image have sent a subtle, unofficial message to the Iranian people that the United States recognized a transition of political will without throwing the Shah under the bus? Would the November 1979 takeover of the US embassy in Tehran by Islamist students have been avoided? We will never know.

From roughly 1927, the year of Pan Am's founding, to approximately 1947, as Pan Am's contributions to the war effort wound down with the end of the Berlin Blockade, Pan Am was considered by the US government as a "chosen instrument" extension of the State Department.

When it suited political needs, Pan Am was seen as the American flag carrier, but as Pan Am competed with foreign and domestic airlines to protect the international markets Pan Am had built from scratch, the government stated, "There is no American flag carrier." Is it possible that in this case, Zbigniew Brzezinski decided that Pan Am was an American flag carrier, and the sight of an American flag on a Pan Am 747 carrying the Ayatollah Khomeini home to Tehran was not convenient to the security of the United States? We will never know.

FLYING THE LINE

PAN AM

Not a Good Idea

The Pan Am 747SP was the longest-distance aircraft in the fleet, flying 6,741 miles nonstop New York to Tokyo and 7,620 miles nonstop New York to Dhahran, Saudi Arabia. The overnight flight to Dhahran took twelve hours, and the staff were trained to accommodate both Western and Muslim customs around food and alcohol or the absence thereof.

About halfway to Dhahran, somewhere over Germany, the purser called the cockpit. "I need help back here with a passenger who has had too many drinks. Now he's trying to take a bottle from—" Then silence. The captain turned to the flight engineer and said, "Go back there and see what the problem is. She doesn't respond on the interphone anymore."

Knowing that the cabin would be dark, he grabbed a six-volt flashlight and walked back to the aft galley as ordered. There he discovered a young Arabian man trying to force the purser away from the beverage cart. When he saw the flight engineer, he backed away from the cart and faced him. The shaken purser said, "He tried to take a bottle of booze from the cart after I told him he could not have another drink. He said no woman could tell him what to do. He snatched the phone from my hand, and that's when I called the cockpit."

The flight engineer instructed the young man, "Sit down and behave yourself, or we will have the police arrest you upon arrival."

"Don't tell me about the police. I am studying to be a policeman in college in California," argued the young man, and then he spit on the flight engineer's arm. Instinctively, the flight engineer slapped him hard across his right ear and threatened to handcuff him if he didn't sit down and shut up. His seatmate, another young Arabian student, jumped up, and yelled, "You hit my friend!"

"That's right. Now you sit down, or you'll get the same. We have about seven hours remaining, and if you two give us any more trouble, I will handcuff both of you. You'll have trouble going to the lavatory and relieving yourselves." They sat down.

Returning to the cockpit, the flight engineer described the problem of excessive alcohol, their displeasure of being cut off, and the outcome of the passengers returning to their seats. The resolving slap across the right ear was not mentioned. Upon arrival in Dhahran, the captain filed a report for the chief pilot, and neither pilot thought much more of the incident.

When they returned to JFK, the operations manager told the captain and flight engineer that the two young men had gone to the Dhahran ticket office to file a complaint that one of them had been assaulted by a crewmember. The ticket office manager called the Dhahran airport operations office and asked what to do. The operations manager said, "I will fax you the crew report." The two young men listened to the report, and then turned and left. Pan Am never heard another word as the two men would need to admit that they had consumed alcohol—not a good idea when complaining in Saudi Arabia.

Above and Beyond

Most Pan Am-ers, when they think about the IGS, as the Internal German Service was known, reflect on the unique feature of that one-of-a-kind operation. Set up by the mandate of the Potsdam Agreement, signed by the three victorious powers at the termination of World War II, the IGS was one of three similar operations set up to provide direct and uninterrupted service to Berlin after hostilities ended. By an unfortunate quirk, the demarcation lines that divided the conquered nation resulted in the placing of the former capital of the Third Reich over 150 miles into the Soviet zone of occupation. Each of the four occupying powers had a piece of Berlin. The United Kingdom and France each established their own air service to and from Berlin from the west, and after the absorption of American Overseas Airlines by Pan Am, the task of providing air service by the Americans fell to Pan American.

I was lucky enough to have been assigned to the IGS for several years. One flight that stands out took place on a sunny Sunday morning on a trip from Berlin to Dusseldorf. I was the first officer. Like all of our skippers, the captain that day was a wonderfully laid-back individual, an exceptional airman, and a great guy to fly with. We had flown together numerous times, and I always enjoyed our trips together. I strolled out to the Boeing 727 sitting gracefully in the morning sun, rear stairs extended, which was just a bit unusual, as they were normally up and stowed prior to any scheduled departure. I was looking forward to a fun day of flying and to the tennis game I had scheduled that afternoon.

I climbed up the airstairs at the front left entry door and entered the main cabin. The three stewardesses greeted me with the news that we were going to be carrying a critically ill passenger to Dusseldorf for medical treatment that wasn't available anywhere else in the country.

The passenger was a very prominent and influential citizen in Berlin and indeed in the country and was being afforded every advantage in the treatment of his affliction. I strolled back to the rear of the aircraft and saw that the rear five rows had been blocked off, and a curtain separated the section from the rest of the cabin. Just before the passengers boarded, an ambulance rolled through the gate and up to the rear airstairs. The patient was carefully carried up the rear stairs and placed atop the folded-down seats, with a doctor and two nurses sitting with him in the row just ahead of the curtain.

The rest of the boarding was routine, and we started engines and blocked out on schedule for the one-hour-and-twenty-minute flight to the Rhineland. It was a beautiful day for flying, and the trip was smooth as glass; we landed a few minutes ahead of schedule. This was before the installation of jetways at many airports, and we parked on the ramp and deplaned using a portable airstair. As we shut the engines down, from my seat I could see the ambulance parked off to the side waiting for the last of the passengers to deplane. Just then the patient's doctor entered the cockpit; we could see that he was in a very agitated state. "Herr Flugkapitain," he said, "we have a serious problem. My patient unfortunately has passed away while enroute to Dusseldorf, and the authorities are preparing to disembark him here. This is a very serious problem for the family!" He clipped his sentences sharply, and his penetrating eyes were those of a man who was used to being obeyed. "It will create great hardship and expense for the family if he is left here. Can you possibly take him back to Berlin? We will leave the stretcher curtained off and quietly let him off in Berlin."

The station manager hovered in the background, insisting that this was strictly against regulations and that Pan American would be severely sanctioned.

The captain and I exchanged glances. "Well, doctor, I'm not sure we are permitted to do that. What do you think, John?"

"I don't have a problem with it. Your call, skipper," I replied.

He thought for a long moment, then turning to the doctor he said, "OK, we will do it. Do what you have to do to keep him aboard." I thought the doctor was going to swoon with gratitude The captain got out of his seat and strode quickly to the aft of the cabin to stop the unloading process. It was an interesting tableau, with the ambulance drivers poised at the top of the aft airstairs and the doctor making himself a physical barrier in front of his patient, and the captain and I watching the whole proceedings. Finally, after much discussion, the station manager and the medics deplaned and the passengers boarded. We closed up and departed for Berlin, each of us wondering just what awaited us when we returned.

We landed at Tempelhof on schedule. Word of our unusual cargo had preceded us, and without fanfare, our unfortunate passenger was offloaded. The skipper and I changed airplanes and went off to our next trip. When we returned to Berlin after our day's flying was done, we had filed the incident in the back of our minds as just another day in the IGS.

The following morning, however, proved that yesterday was not as innocent as we thought. The same captain and I were paired again on this day, and when I checked in at operations for the day's trips, I was told by the operations supervisor that my presence was requested in the chief pilot's office at once. When I walked into his office, I could see through the open door that the captain was already there. The secretary motioned me into the office with a bemused grin on her face. The chief pilot was a really good guy, like almost everyone in the IGS, but he reamed us out that morning. "What in blazes were you thinking?" he asked. "Do you have any idea how many rules and regulations you busted, to say nothing of the German laws?" He went on at great length about how we could be thrown in jail and Pan American given a severe black eye.

We both stood rigidly planted in front of his desk. The skipper finally spoke up. "Chief, it seemed like a humanitarian thing to do at the time."

There was a long pause. A small grin tickled at the corner of the chief's mouth. He reached into the pile of papers on his desk and handed us a copy of that day's *Berliner Zeitung*, the local equivalent to the New York Daily News. We both knew enough German to see immediately that we were notorious. Splashed across the front page was a banner story about the great good deed that had been done by Pan Am and its gallant pilots the day before, a detailed accounting of our escapade to Dusseldorf, and that the skipper and I, and Pan Am, were granted hero status.

"Just don't do it again," the chief said. "Now get the hell out of here!"

Reprinted with permission of Captain John Marshall

What Goes Around, Comes Around

Whether by accident or design, almost everyone who worked for Pan Am had a healthy sense of humor and weren't shy to pull pranks on each other. Perhaps no one did it better than the flight crews. Whether it was the close proximity of working together on flight decks, small kitchen galleys, and narrow aircraft aisles, and the long hours of flying together, a physical gag or prank was hard to resist.

The first such victims were the "newbies." In the late sixties, this new flight attendant, fresh out of training and eager to please, was assigned to the 707 first-class section. In addition to serving first-class customers, the flight attendants were responsible for serving the flight deck crew consisting of the captain, first officer, flight engineer, and navigator. The 707 flight deck was small and crowded. The newbie flight attendant knocked on the cabin door, opened it, and walked in with a tray of hot coffee. As the navigator was standing to take a sextant reading on the stars, the engineer reached over and tapped the navigator in his privates with a ruler. The navigator, also a newbie, yelped and turned to face the hapless flight attendant. Without missing a beat, the crafty engineer exclaimed, "What's your hurry, dear? You don't even know if he's married." The flight attendant turned bright red as the flight deck crew howled in laughter.

Understanding the initiation, the flight attendant returned to the first-class galley, not to be outdone. She bided her time patiently until the prankster engineer exited the cabin and went into the nearby lavatory. A first-class older woman got up from her seat and asked for the lavatory.

The flight attendant quietly unlocked the lavatory in use. Nonplussed, the woman said to the engineer's back, "Take your time, dearie. Just let me know when you're done."

"What the hell?" was heard as the door was quietly closed and relocked.

Welcome Aboard

As Pan Am introduced the world to the new age of jet travel with their 707 and DC8 four-engine jet aircraft, the renowned first-class epicurean experience created by Pan Am during the Presidential Service of the late fifties on their Boeing 377 Stratocruisers were now upgraded again in partnership with the famous catering kitchens of Maxim's in Paris. Back then, Pan Am delivered a fine dining experience instead of what is known today as a meal service.

First class travel in the sixties was affordable primarily by government officials, celebrities, and wealthy families. Many of Pan Am's wealthy patrons originated overseas, and if one was wealthy in South America, that was another level of wealth that often came with cultural differences not shared by American society.

On board this evening's flight from Buenos Aires to Miami was a young couple, the husband immaculately tailored in a bespoke light gray suit and his wife beautifully coiffed in her fashionable Coco Chanel suit with jewelry intended to impress.

The lead first-class flight attendant and flight purser was among Pan Am's most experienced and polished veterans, and she quickly recognized the couple as VIP passengers who could have flown first-class on their native country flag carrier, Aerolineas Argentinas, but chose Pan Am for the superior inflight experience.

Smiling, she welcomed the couple by name and handed each the large first-class menu, which outlined on two pages the full dining experience: starting with choice of aperitifs and cocktails, followed by the caviar service, then a choice of appetizers, main course entrees, and finishing with desserts, cheese plates, and a selection of ports.

Allowing enough time for the passengers to peruse the menu, the flight attendant returned to the VIP couple and asked the woman first, "Madam, what may I bring you as a cocktail?"

The woman did not acknowledge the question and continued to flip the pages of her fashion magazine.

"My wife will have a Manhattan," answered the husband, "and I will have a very dry martini."

Following cocktails and the caviar service, with chilled vodka, the flight attendant inquired, "Madam, what may I serve you as appetizers?" Again, no response as she looked out the window. "We'll both have the Mayan prawns," instructed the husband.

Puzzled by the wife's behavior, the flight attendant thought perhaps the wife did not speak English. When it was time to order the main entree, she asked the wife, "Señora, ¿qué le gusta de plato principal?" This time, the wife looked up as if she would respond but took another bite of the Mayan prawn instead.

The husband interceded, "Young lady, while your Spanish is excellent, you don't seem to understand. In our home, my wife does not interact with the servants."

The flight attendant thought for a moment, smiled, and responded politely, "Yes, sir, I understand that's the custom in your home. But this Pan American first-class cabin is my home, and your wife is my guest."

When the Job Was Fun

At the conclusion of World War II, commercial air transportation between West Germany and the isolated city of Berlin was controlled by the occupying armies of the United Kingdom, France, and the United States. The German airline, Lufthansa, was forbidden air rights to Berlin.

The three airlines certified for service in 1945 were British European Airways (BEA), Air France, and American Overseas Airlines (AOA), a subsidiary of American Airlines, who hoped to use AOA as a means of getting into the international markets. But by 1948, W. R. Smith, chairman of American Airlines, tired of the mounting losses of AOA, and AOA was happily acquired by Pan Am. The acquisition was originally denied by the Civil Aeronautics Board, but that decision was overturned by President Truman as a probable bone thrown to Pan Am for the constant denial of Pan Am's request for domestic routes within the United States.

In 1950, Pan Am became the US carrier for the Inter German Service (IGS), and profitably serviced the German market for the next 40 years until its sale to Lufthansa in October 1990.

With the fall of the Berlin Wall on November 9, 1989, and the ultimate unification of Germany, the need for an IGS service became superfluous. Considering the financial hemorrhaging of Pan Am between 1980 and 1991, the cash sale to Lufthansa for $150 million was fortuitous.

The IGS was a profitable and unique subsidiary of Pan Am. West Berlin was an island of allied occupation and Western democracy, isolated in the communist sea of East Germany. Rail and ground transportation between West Germany and West Berlin was highly limited and restricted by the Soviet Union. The three air corridors assigned to BEA, Air France, and Pan Am were limited to 9,000 feet eastbound, 10,000 feet westbound, and a width of 20 miles. The speed of travel and frequency of passenger and freight flights was West Berlin's lifeline.

The challenges of flying in narrow air corridors, while occasionally harassed by Soviet MIGs, and finally landing in the inner city Tempelhof Airport via a challenging approach between two massive housing towers in the lowest possible bad weather ceiling made the IGS assignment not for the faint of heart. Additionally, while Berliners enjoyed an anything-goes social playground atmosphere, it was still a long way from the amenities of home. As a result, the closeknit band of brothers who piloted at day and partied at night enjoyed a "Home Alone" type freedom, with an almost benign neglect by supervision from headquarters. As long as the IGS delivered record profits, high passenger yields, and on-time performances without any significant damage or loss of life, headquarters turned a blind eye to the long hair, sideburns, bombardier jackets, and gags of the fraternity.

In many ways, the IGS was run similarly to a modern-day startup. People had fun but produced a great product. Customers loved them, particularly the Pan Am crews' willingness to bend the rules to satisfy customer needs. The flight is full and the German businessman needs to get home to Berlin for his daughter's birthday? Go sit in the flight attendant jump seat. The fight is full and the Pan Am gate agent's father is in the hospital in Frankfurt? Take the check pilot's seat in the cockpit.

In 1975, things started to change. Operations moved from Templehof, whose runways were limited to 6,000 feet, to the suburbs of Tegel Airport, whose 9,000-foot runways could accommodate the heavier jets and longer-range aircraft. With the onset of the oil embargo and skyrocketing fuel prices, in 1973, the profitability of the IGS division became very slim. By 1980, the new Pan Am chairman, C. Edward Acker, decided they could fly their way out of financial trouble and expanded both the IGS routes, plus opened additional routes from the Frankfurt hub to Scandinavia, Eastern Europe, and the Mediterranean.

Eastern Europe did well, as many of the passengers were guest workers, which Germany then welcomed to fuel its growth.

But history is not always kind to those who serve it well. With the 1989 fall of the Berlin Wall and unification of Germany, Pan Am lost its inter-German monopoly that had been well subsidized by the West German government. The December 1988 bombing over Lockerbie, plus the sale of Atlantic routes to United and Delta in 1991, led to the ultimate demise of Pan Am on December 4, 1991.

Nevertheless, the IGS division was a unique and beloved part of Pan Am history. Ask any former IGS pilot what it was like flying the line back then, and you'll usually get a rueful smile and the comment, "Oh, yeah. That was quite a time."

Can't You See?

If you were an international Pan Am flight attendant, there were two things that were true. One, friends you made "flying the line" around the world, were most likely friends for life long after you left the airline;and two, based on managing sensitive customers onboard, and shopping the bazaars around the world - you were a master negotiator and thought quickly on your feet.

Two such Pan Am friends, now enjoying their retirement years, have a standing date to meet once a week to walk their dogs, have lunch, and share gossip. Each have two very different dogs: a German Shepherd and a Chihuahua.

It's about 12 noon on a clear sunny day, and the first flight attendant says, "Hey, there's that new Italian restaurant everyone's talking about. Let's go there for lunch."

"We can't go there," replies her friend. "There is no outdoor seating, and they won't allow dogs in the restaurant."

"Sure, they will."

"How are you going to do that?"

"Look, I was a Pan Am purser. I know how to get things done," she instructs as she puts on her sunglasses . "Wear your sunglasses, and follow my lead. Just do what I do and say what I say."

With their two leashed dogs leading the way, they approach the maitre d'. "Hello young man," greets the German Shepherd owner, "We have heard wonderful things about your new restaurant, and would like to have lunch."

"I'm sorry, madam," apologized the maitre d' "but we don't allow dogs in the restaurant."

Staring straight ahead through her sunglasses, she protests, "Young man…can't you see that I am visually impaired, and this is my seeing eye dog?" The German Shepherd looks up at the maitre d' in obvious agreement.

"Oh, my dear, I apologize. I didn't realize. We have a lovely table for you. Please step this way."

After seating the first friend, together with the German Shepherd, he returns to the restaurant entrance to find the remaining friend waiting. "Yes, may I help you?," asks the maitre d'.

"I wish to join my friend for lunch, as she requested."

"I'm sorry, madam. As I explained to your companion, we do not allow dogs in the restaurant unless they are service animals."

Following her friend's lead, she stares straight ahead through her sunglasses. "Young man, isn't it obvious that I too am visually impaired, and this is my seeing eye dog?"

The maitre d' looks down at the diminutive chihuahua smiling back at him.

"Madam," he says as politely as possible. "This isn't a seeing eye dog… it's a chihuahua."

"What?" she shrieks in reply." You mean to tell me they gave me a chihuahua?"

ANIMAL CRACKERS

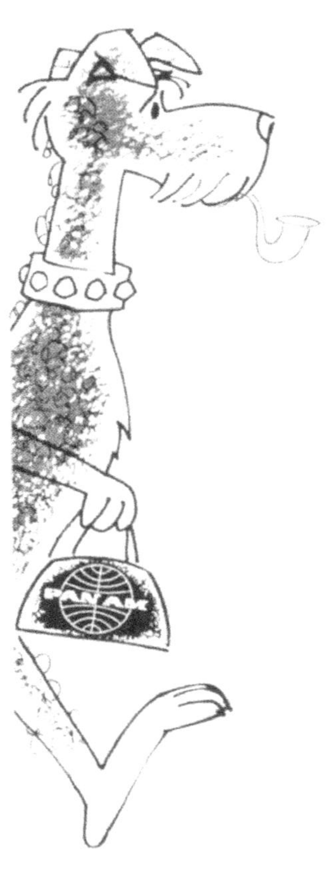
PAN AM

Best of Intentions

Pan Am's passengers consisted often of international expatriates moving to or from an international destination for a multiyear assignment. After a two-year assignment in San Francisco, a petroleum engineer for British Petroleum was returning to her home in the United Kingdom and booked travel for herself and her dog, a tan and white Cavalier King Charles Spaniel.

Pan Am transported thousands of animals, from household dogs and cats, to rhesus monkeys, to tigers and elephants. It was everyone's greatest fear that any animal would arrive damaged or dead.

Upon arrival at Heathrow Airport in London, it was customary for cargo animals to be unloaded by Pan Am cargo handlers before moving to the Heathrow Animal Reception Centre, where, historically, they were quarantined for six months. Upon opening the cargo door, the Pan Am handlers unloaded the dog crate only to find a deceased Cavalier King Charles Spaniel.

"Blimey," exclaimed the cargo supervisor. "How could this happen? He was secured in the pressurized compartment. There's plenty of food and water. This can't happen."

They looked at the clock and knew that the owner would require about two hours to clear customs on her own, collect her luggage, and find her way over to the cargo hangar. Besides managing the grief of the passenger, the last thing they needed was an official inquiry with a lot of questions they couldn't answer and paperwork to complete. What to do?

"You know," slowly suggested one handler, "I've got a mate at home who is moving from their house into a small flat and is selling an adult

Spaniel who looks identical to this one. I could run over and bring him back within the hour." The supervisor, known for not being bound by regulations in the service manuals, and for finding the shortest distance between two points, nodded and said, "Go do it."

Sure enough, the BP petroleum engineer appeared and asked to see her dog. Upon being presented with the crate with a very live Cavalier King Charles Spaniel, the passenger burst into tears and cried, "This isn't my dog."

"Are you sure, madam? The manifest lists a tan and brown Cavalier King Charles Spaniel, and that's what we have here."

"No, no, no," sobs the bereaved passenger. "My spaniel is dead. He was dying of cancer in San Francisco, so we put him down before coming home and intended to bury him in our garden in Woking. Where is my dog?"

The road to hell is paved with good intentions, and this was such a journey. Sheepishly and apologetically, the Pan Am supervisor admitted that they assumed the dead dog was their fault and attempted, inappropriately but without malice, to correct the situation.

Angry but relieved that her original dog had not been lost, the BP petroleum engineer departed with her beloved pet—as well as the successor Cavalier King Charles Spaniel, who found a new home.

Put the Dog Down

It was a quiet Sunday evening at the Pan Am Rate Desk in San Francisco. The Rate Desk was a division of the Pan Am reservation department whose agents calculated the price of individual international tickets based on the unique itinerary of the traveler. One-way and roundtrip journeys were published fares, easy for a reservation agent to quote from the Panamac computer, but journeys that involved two or more stops in a circular itinerary had no published fare, and the ticket price had to be "constructed" by hand using a combination of tariff rules and mileage flown. The rate agent would literally map out the journey on a large white sheet of paper, determine the mileage between points, base the final ticket price on the fare to the furthest point with possible mileage supplements, and check the tariff rules for any discrepancies. It was the tariff rules that caused tonight's crisis.

The call came in from the Seattle airport where Pan Am agents were checking in passengers for that evening's flight to London.

"Pan Am Rate Desk, good evening. How may I help you," answered the rate agent.

"Hi, there, Doris, SEA-TAC here," replied the airport agent. "I have a customer here whose itinerary from Seattle to Frankfurt via JFK was canceled, and reservations were rebooked for her and her dog via London. I need to know what the new fare will be."

"Well, that's a problem. The dog can't transition to the UK without a twenty-four-hour quarantine, which will require a stop in London, and London is a fare HIP to Frankfurt."

"What's a fare HIP?" questioned the airport agent.

"Higher Intermediate Point, meaning that the fare to London is higher than the fare to Frankfurt, so a traveler has to pay the higher fare to stop in London."

"OK, then, what's the new fare?"

"Give me a minute." The rate agent placed the call on hold.

"SEA-TAC, you'll need to collect an eight-hundred-dollar surcharge in order to reticket via London."

"What?! Are you crazy? I can't ask her to pay an extra eight hundred dollars because we canceled her original itinerary."

"I'm sorry, but those are the fare rules. If she wasn't traveling with the dog, she could transit London the same day for the same fare."

"Hold on," instructed the airport. "I'll let her know."

Five minutes passed; the airport agent came back on the line. "She refuses to pay the surcharge. What do I tell her to do?"

The rate desk agent thought for a moment. It had been a quiet but long Sunday night shift; his New York gallows humor got the better of him. "Tell her to put the dog down, get on the flight, and get a new dog in Frankfurt or her final destination."

There was a stunned silence on the telephone. Finally, a soft voice asked, "You're not serious, are you?"

"No, no, no, I was just kidding," reassured the rate agent. "For God's sake, don't tell her that; she will lose her cookies. Hold on a second. Let me check the flights in Panamac." He returned to the call. "Book her on the United redeye tonight from Seattle to JFK, connecting to Pan Am 100 leaving tomorrow morning for Frankfurt. You can reticket that at the same fare."

"Fine, thank you," sighed the airport agent, and they signed off.

Just another day at the Pan Am Rate Desk, thought the agent, remembering the advice of his sage aunt: "Where there's a will … there's a relative."

White Tigers

The cargo department of Pan Am, known as Clipper Cargo, started in 1942 with the carriage of war materials and related goods during World War II. Total tonnage increased exponentially after the war and continued to grow with the fleet of all cargo freighters of 747s and 747 SPs. Clipper Cargo ceased all freighter operations in 1982 as aircraft were sold off as "expendable assets" in a never-ending financial need to keep the passenger services running.

In its heyday, Clipper Cargo was famous for transporting everything from Ferraris to ferrets. It was almost the Barnum & Bailey of airborne freight. Due to Pan Am's global network, Clipper Cargo could transport exotic animals from Africa, Asia, and the Indian subcontinent. In this instance, Clipper Cargo flight was inbound from Karachi with two white tigers purchased by the famous tiger- and lion-training team of Siegfried and Roy. Clipper Cargo schedules did not coincide with passenger schedules. This flight arrived about 2 a.m. and was scheduled to depart again at 6 a.m.

Siegfried and Roy were dedicated to the welfare of their animals. Despite the late night arrival, Siegfried was waiting at the Clipper Cargo hanger to ensure the well-being of their tigers. While one of two tigers arrived easily within its cage, the second tiger had managed to escape its cage. Thirsty, jet lagged, and terrified, the loose tiger was not about to cooperate. No number of brave Clipper Cargo teamsters were going to "shoo" this animal back into the crate.

Supervisors called the Bronx Zoo, the Central Park Zoo, and the Humane Society and SPCA seeking assistance in the form of, if nothing else, a tranquilizer gun. Being three o'clock in the morning, no one answered the phone. They then called the New York City Animal and Control center. Here, someone answered the phone but told the Pan Am supervisor that the issue, being airport based, belonged to the Port of New York and New Jersey.

By now, the noise and furor had raised the attention of the Port Authority Police Department. The station chief arrived at the scene and was not pleased that he was called away from his desk (or nap) at this late hour. He was a George Patton–like veteran of thirty-five years, and he deliberately chose the graveyard shift as an easy means to punch the clock down to retirement.

After assessing the situation, he barked, "Who owns this animal?"

"Zat would be me," volunteered Siegfried. "I am Siegried."

"Mr 'Stinkfeed,' you have a problem."

"Siegfried."

"Whatever. This animal is a lethal danger to these workers and needs to be controlled and contained. If you can't accomplish that in the next hour, I will put this tiger down myself, and it will appear on a Chinatown menu tomorrow evening."

"That preposterous," replied Siegfried. "You can not do dat."

"What? I can't do that? Hey, I've got a badge and a gun. What do you got?"

Siegfried looked back blankly

"My shift ends in an hour and a half. You have exactly one hour to get that animal back into its cage. I suggest you get a whip and a chair and whatever mumbo jumbo German you use to talk to the thing and get started. When I come back, I better hear a cat purring and not a tiger roaring."

And with that, the station captain turned sharply on his heels and left the building.

It's not clear if Siegfried actually had with him a whip and a chair or if he improvised with a belt and a broom, but he eventually managed to coax the tiger back to his cage. The tiger was deplaned and processed through customs, and the Pan Am Clipper freighter returned to its appointed cargo rounds on schedule.

You Ought to Be in Pictures

Back in the "Mad Men" advertising days of the sixties and early seventies, if the door to a job as a Pan Am flight attendant was a young woman's poise, personality, and professionalism, then her good looks were the key that unlocked the door. Being of model-like beauty wasn't enough to keep the job; she had to maintain the same standards of waist and weight that she measured on her day of hire throughout her employment. To police that policy, flight attendant supervisors would conduct periodic, unannounced "weight checks" as flight attendants reported for their flight. Fortunately, those bigoted standards are now of a bygone age.

None of those burdens were initially of concern to the excited young candidates as they underwent training at the Pan Am regional headquarters training academy adjacent to Miami Airport. The combined administrative and training facility was a beautifully ornate Maharaja palace-like campus, affectionately known as the Taj Mahal.

Many beautiful women had worked as models and decided to exchange the fashion runways for airline runways in search of travel and glamor. It was not unusual for Pan Am PR photographers to single out certain women to be part of a publicity photo shoot. One new hire was selected with the following invitation.

"Would you be willing to be part of a PR photo shoot tomorrow after training class?"

"Sure, what's the occasion?"

"We have a VIP transiting Miami on his way to South America, and we would like to get a few photos of him and a beautiful Pan Am flight attendant like you."

"Is he a movie star?"

"Not exactly, although he could appear in movies—probably movies about animals from Africa."

"Is he like a Tarzan type?"

"Well, not exactly. He's more like the strong, silent type. His name is George."

"What time tomorrow afternoon should I report? I assume at the Pan Am terminal?"

"Tomorrow at 4:00 p.m. Report to the cargo hangar."

"Cargo hangar?"

"Yeah, cargo hangar. It will make sense when you report."

The following day, the eager flight attendant, beautifully resplendent in her Evan-Picone uniform, reported to the cargo hangar office.

"I'm here for my photoshoot with George," she announced to the cargo supervisor.

"George who?"

"I'm not sure. I was told by the PR photographer to show up today to do a photo shoot with a VIP traveler transiting Miami to South America."

"Ohhh, *that* George," replied the supervisor with a smile that turned into a mischievous grin. "Come with me." He escorted her past various cargo containers, oil drums, and pallets stacked high with cargo wrapped in rope netting back to the rear of the cargo hangar to an area whose aroma reminded one of a zoo.

"Ah, there you are," welcomed the photographer. "Meet George."

George was, in fact, a VIP. He was an 1,800-pound, two-year-old elephant, imported from Africa via Miami and destined by Pan Am to the Guyana Zoological Park in Georgetown, Guyana. He was standing in a staged bed of hay with the Pan Am logo tented behind him.

The photographer handed the flabbergasted flight attendant a white Pan Am flight bag. It was full of unshelled peanuts. "Hold the bag near his snout." She did, and George gladly stuck his snout in and out of the bag as he fed happily. "Keep smiling," encouraged the photographer.

The photoshoot was part of an advertising campaign to promote Pan Am Clipper Cargo services. While not exactly the glamor anticipated, the photos got picked up by the API and UPI wire services, and, as we say today, "went viral." For years afterward, as the flight attendant worked different flights around the globe, one or more passengers would ask, "Are you that famous model with the Pan Am elephant?"

PAN AM

END OF AN ERA

PAN AM

The Last Clipper

The Pan Am Clippers was a nomenclature chosen by Juan Trippe to define speed and elegance. The term was taken to mirror in aircraft the mid-nineteenth-century merchant sailing vessels designed for speed on the high seas between the continents of Europe, Asia, and the Americas. Each Pan Am airboat vessel and land aircraft were named after clipper ships that preceded them.

Air traffic controllers always use the airline name and flight numbers as identifiers. Only two airlines were identified by formal names: "Skybird" for Imperial, now British Airways, and "Clipper" for Pan Am.

In January 1991, Pan Am filed for bankruptcy protection and continued to operate on financial fumes, fueled mostly by cash infusions from Delta Airlines in the hope that Pan Am could re-emerge as a slimmed-down version of itself and serve the markets where it had originated in 1927: the Caribbean and Central America. On December 3, the day the new Pan Am was scheduled to shed its Chapter Eleven protection, Delta lawyer Lawrence M. Handelsman told the bankruptcy court that Delta had decided not to pump any more money into Pan Am.

On December 4, in Barbados, sitting in the cockpit of the Boeing 727 Clipper Goodwill, Captain Mark Pyle watched the Pan Am station manager walking toward the airplane. Pyle could tell by the manager's face that it was bad news. All the news those days was bad. Pyle and his crew already knew before they left New York that Delta Airlines had withdrawn from the restructured Pan Am deal. The news was only bound to get worse. Pyle read the Teletype message the manager handed him. In curt language, it declared that as of nine o'clock that morning the airline had ceased operations. Pyle went back to the cabin to tell the flight attendants. Each of the women had been flying for

Pan Am, or for National, for over twenty years. They all broke down in tears. The manager wanted to know if they would fly the airplane back to Miami. He said he would find a way to buy fuel. Not only were their revenue passengers stranded there in Barbados, many of the now-unemployed Pan Am staff wanted to return to the United States. For Pyle it would be one of his last Pan Am decisions. He was a new captain, and he'd waited eighteen years to get there. He was a former instructor, now a check pilot, and a dedicated company man. He liked to run his airplane by the book.

"How long will it take?" he asked.

"Maybe two hours."

Pyle had to laugh. What could they do? Fire him? "We'll wait," he said. "We'll wait as long as it takes."

Two hours later, when the passengers and employees were aboard, they took off for Miami. A hundred miles out, the flight engineer, Chuck Freeman, made radio contact with Pan Am operations. Then he turned to the captain. He was choking back tears. "Mark, we're the last flight. . . the final flight. They want us to make a low pass." Another decision, probably his last. Low pass? And then it occurred to him: This is a historic moment. A low pass? Absolutely. So that's what he did. Low. He brought Clipper Goodwill right down the centerline of runway 12, low enough for the folks on the ground to count the rivets. They turned downwind, landed, and taxied toward the gate. It was like a victory parade. Vehicles—police, fire trucks, security cars, tow trucks— lined the taxiway. Television crews followed the taxiing airplane. Ramp workers came to attention and saluted. Water cannons fired streams over the slowly moving jetliner. All the Pan Am personnel at the gate were standing at attention as Pyle brought the jet to a stop. Pyle shook hands with Chuck Freeman and Bob Knox, the twenty-three-year veteran first officer. They had just flown the final trip of a Pan American Clipper.

Reprinted by permission of Robert Gandt, author of *SkyGods: The Fall of Pan Am*

Master of the Ship

The hotel room telephone jangled the captain out of a sound sleep. He had piloted the Pan Am 747 from New York to Sao Paulo and had hoped for a decent day's rest before flying the return flight the evening of December 4, 1991.

On the other end of the line was the Pan Am Director for South America, whose manner was brusque and short. "Captain, effective 0900 New York time, Pan Am has ceased operations. Your aircraft is turning around in Montevideo immediately and will be back in Sao Paulo by 3:00 p.m. You must contact your crew and any others who may be at the hotel. I suggest you contact the local station manager to make the arrangements. The airplane must be away by dark."

And there it was, starkly in front of him like a corpse. After a year operating in bankruptcy protection, selling their venerable European routes to United and Delta Airlines, and flying on the fumes of a financial promise from Delta to invest into a restructured Pan Am known as Pan II, Delta's lawyers abandoned their bride at the bankruptcy court altar on December 3 with the apology, "We're sorry, your Honor. The world has changed." Commitment had given way to expediency.

Gently laying the telephone back in the cradle, the captain's first thoughts were *Now what do I do?* After twenty-nine years of dedicated service, his family was suddenly without income or medical insurance. That would have to wait. As captain, his first responsibility was to his family of crew members and the security of his aircraft, the 747 bearing the nautical name Clipper Nautilus. In the maritime tradition upon which Pan Am was originally built with the first flying Sikorsky Flying Boats, he was the master of the ship, a position of honor and ultimate authority in which he was responsible for the safety and success of his crew, passengers, and cargo. No one could usurp the authority of the master, including the owners, as evidenced in modern times when the chairman of Pan Am attempted to command a 747 captain to depart the gate despite a leak in the hydraulic system, not yet repaired.

"I happen to be the CEO of this airline, and I'm telling you to get this goddamn airplane out of here."

"I happen to be the captain of this airplane," replied the master, "and this airplane will depart when I am satisfied that it is airworthy. Not before."

There wasn't much time to collect the crew. Fortunately, Sao Paulo was not one of the great shopping bargains of the world, so it wasn't difficult to find the flight attendants still in the hotel. Two hours later, flight attendants and pilots crowded into the crew bus and drove back to the airport. The atmosphere was quiet, interrupted with tears of disbelief. Disembarking at the terminal was no better. The body of the company was not even cold, yet all the signs bearing the airline's name had mysteriously disappeared, counters were deserted, computers unplugged and stacked haphazardly wherever there was space. The 747, instead of parked at the terminal next to other international aircraft, had been shunted off to an obscure corner of the airfield as if in shame.

Fueled and catered to accommodate the two crews dead heading back to New York, Clipper Nautilus departed in the afternoon of the Brazilian summer and headed back to the winter weather and bleak reality in New York. The crew, plus one lonely pass rider, a mother of a Pan Am employee, occupied the first-class cabin and tried to make the best of the first-class catering. Conversation was muted, sad, somber, and tearful. Everyone felt like Clipper Nautilus was the hearse transporting them to their funeral.

Eleven hours later, the captain started the descent into New York. It was a cold but brilliantly clear night, with the lights of Manhattan standing out like a bright beacon at two o'clock in the morning. As the Captain received the final landing directions from the flight controllers, the conversation was as businesslike as any normal flight—until the controller paused and said quietly, "Welcome home, Clipper. You're the last one."

The arrival was as ignominious as their departure. Unlike the last commercial Pan Am flight from Barbados to Miami that landed in the daytime to a salute of water canons, TV reporters, and Pan Am employees, there was no one to welcome this ship home. Only a lonely parking spot outside the International Arrivals Building where they were greeted by one lone Delta maintenance agent whose sole contribution was to install the gear pins and wheel a maintenance ladder up to the left forward door—and then disappeared.

With twenty-nine years seniority, the captain did not need to go down with the fleet. He could have jumped ship and moved to United in 1986 when they purchased the Pacific routes from Pan Am. He could have moved to Delta in 1990 when they acquired the European routes. But he stayed because Pan Am had something more important: Pan Am was to aviation what NASA was to space. It was the major leagues of international aviation, and he wasn't about to go to the minor leagues where a captain was captain in name only, where decisions were made only upon the approval of headquarters, compared to the ultimate authority of being the master of the ship. His career, like all Pan Am masters, was built on fulfilling the success of the mission versus following the book, and as he shut down the engines of Clipper Nautilus and turned out the lights, that's how he ended it: as the master of the ship.

PANAM

EPILOGUE

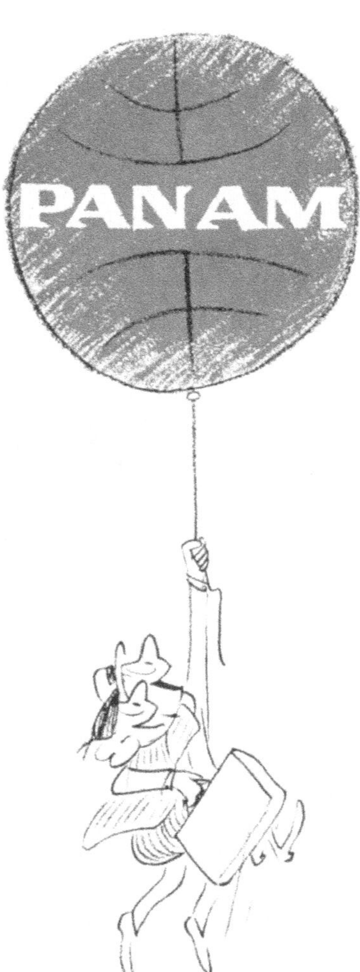

PAN AM

Gone but Not Forgotten

Pan Am had a short corporate life relative to its global icon compatriots IBM and Coca-Cola, and yet, Pan Am impacted the globe as much as its companions in ways that still exist today.

So why isn't Pan Am still here?

Pan Am's struggles and demise were driven by a combination of bad government, bad decisions, and bad luck.

Juan Trippe, one of the original founders of Pan Am, was in his day a combination of Elon Musk, Steve Jobs, and Bill Gates. Juan Trippe created for aviation what Elon Musk did for electric cars, Steve Jobs did for personal computers, and Bill Gates did for software. They all created products and technology that still influence global commerce today. Like Musk, Jobs, and Gates, Juan Trippe was driven in his vision and passion for what aviation would bring to the world. As Juan Trippe built a global network of commercial aviation by connecting the United States by air to South America and Asia first, and then Europe, the United States government was content to ride Pan Am's coattails internationally by considering Pan Am a partner to the State Department and an unofficial chosen instrument of United States diplomacy. Additionally, during World War II, Pan Am turned over all their B-314 and Martin flying boats to the US Navy and Army Air Force, trained navigators and engineers for military duty, and ferried essential supplies and aircraft via South America and West Africa to the allied forces in North Africa, Middle East, and India. Pan Am believed that patriotism had its rewards. Unfortunately, while the State and War Departments were supporters of Pan Am, Presidents Roosevelt, Truman, Eisenhower, and Kennedy were not.

Furthermore, Juan Trippe was a strong personality and not shy to go over the bureaucratic heads of government to get his way. Over time, the bureaucrats of the Civil Aeronautics Board considered Pan Am a monopoly in the international aviation market and protected domestic carriers by prohibiting Pan Am from having the right to carry passengers within the United States. By the time the industry was deregulated in 1978 and Pan Am acquired domestic routes by purchasing National Airlines, it was too little, too late. Adding to Pan Am's burden, foreign flag carriers from war-torn nations of Europe and Asia (Lufthansa, Air France, KLM, Japan Airlines, among many others) were awarded rights to the same Pan Am routes to and from the United States as part of the Marshall Plan reconstruction efforts. By the end of the 70s foreign flag carriers were transporting more passengers than all US carriers combined

From the airline's founding in 1927 and through his retirement in 1968, Juan Trippe had the Midas touch relative to expansion and investment decisions. In 1966, Pan Am signed a contract with Boeing to design and build the 747, the aircraft that changed international air travel from an experience only for the well-heeled leisure and expense account business traveler to an opportunity for the average middle-class family and student to experience the world. Launched in 1970, the 747 was going to be the affordable magic carpet to shrink the world.

But then, bad luck struck. During the 1973 Arab–Israeli War, Arab members of the Organization of Petroleum Exporting Countries (OPEC) imposed an embargo against the United States in retaliation for the US decision to resupply the Israeli military. Aviation fuel, the life blood of the 747, first doubled, then tripled in cost following the oil embargo. President Nixon introduced price controls in the United States, including aviation fuel, which benefited US airlines, but not Pan Am who purchased 85% of its fuel overseas where prices had tripled from 15 cents a gallon to 44 cents overnight in 1973

Additionally, the surge of terrorist attacks and hijackings on Pan Am and other US-based airlines drove consumers away from international travel, resulting in Pan Am flying near empty 747s around the world at inflated fuel prices, resulting in massive losses. Additionally, Pan Am executives gambled that Pan Am could fly its way out of financial turbulence and invested into an order of long range 747SPs that could fly from New York to Tokyo or Saudi Arabia non-stop. Pan Am retrenched by reducing its global workforce from 43,000 to 28,000 and eliminated unprofitable routes, mostly in the Caribbean. s. Ultimately, Pan Am was forced to sell valuable assets, up to and including the profitable Pacific Division, just to meet payroll and expenses.

Through the 1980s, Pan Am employees persevered and shared the financial pain through wage concessions, employee stock ownership plans, and a reduced pay scale for new hires. As a result, it appeared that Pan Am was going to turn the corner—until bad luck struck yet again. The terrorist bomb explosion of Pan Am 103 over Lockerbie, Scotland, in 1988 initiated the nailing of the coffin, which ended with the termination of operations on December 4, 1991.

Pan Am was not the only airline to declare bankruptcy in the nineties and beyond, yet others survived. Could Pan Am have survived? Not likely. Imagine if the government told Elon Musk that he could manufacture electric cars but never gas-powered cars; that Steve Jobs could manufacture personal computers but not write software; and that Bill Gates could write software but not manufacture personal computers. Pan Am was based on a business model that worked well as a regulated utility whose increased costs and political restrictions could be borne by the consumer but not as a restricted competitor in an open marketplace.

Fortunately, the appetite to preserve the history and aviation legacy of Pan Am runs long and deep. While the population of Pan Am veterans shrinks year by year, the memories stay strong though international and local reunions and through the memberships of these stalwart organizations:

The Pan Am Museum Foundation	https://www.thepanammuseum.org
The Pan Am Historical Foundation	https://www.panam.org

| World Wings International | https://www.worldwingsinternational.net/ |
| Clipper Pioneers | https://www.clipperpioneers.com |

It is the sincere hope of this author that the readers of this book will support one or more of the above organizations to learn more about the great history of Pan Am and to ensure that such history is preserved for future generations.

About the Author

Ace Gilbert's career in the travel industry started with Pan Am. Initially denied a job as a flight attendant with the requisite second language skill ("Mr. Gilbert, your German is about good enough to find the toilet"), he was later hired by Pan Am as a reservation and rate desk agent in New York before transferring to San Francisco where he worked until Pan Am closed in 1991. His career then moved to corporate travel sales and account management for various travel management companies such as Thomas Cook, BCD Travel, and Carlson Wagonlit, before retiring from American Express Global Business Travel.

In addition to writing, Ace Gilbert is the chief listening officer for the advisory firm Advisory Options and produces personal interviews with people of interest titled *15 Minutes of Fame*, which can be found on YouTube. Ace and his therapy dog, Roman, volunteer with the SFO Airport WAG Brigade, offering canine therapy to grateful airport employees and hassled travelers. He resides in Brisbane, California, with his wife, Carol, and their menagerie of dogs, cat, freshwater fish, and wild birds.